EARTHSTARS

THE GEOMETRIC GROUNDPLAN UNDERLYING LONDON'S ANCIENT
SACRED SITES AND ITS SIGNIFICANCE FOR THE NEW AGE

C.E.STREET

HERMITAGE PUBLISHING

ISBN 0 9515967

First published in Britain, 1990, by Hermitage Publishing, P.O. Box 1383, London N14 6LF.

© Copyright: Christopher E. Street, 1990.

Typesetting and page layouts produced at Neal's Yard DTP Studio, London WC2.

Printed by the Scorpion Press, Vestry Estate, Sevenoaks, Kent, TN14 5ET.

To Mother Earth and all her children.

With thanks to John Michell and all the other early pioneers of the Earth Mysteries movement whose groundwork made this book possible.

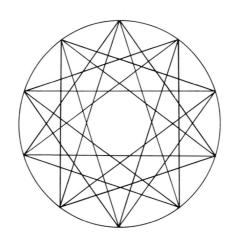

CONTENTS.

ILLUSTRATIONS.

FOREWORD

by

John Michell

The mystery of London goes back to the earliest times, for no-one knows when or how the city was founded. Its legendary history begins in about 1200B.C. when Brutus and an army of Trojans landed in Totnes and having defeated the native giants, occupied London and made it the capital of their realm. Their name for it, New Troy, was still current when Caesar invaded in 54 B.C. for the people he found in possession of London were called the Tri-Novates or New Trojans.

The dynasty of Trojan rulers after Brutus is chronicled into the early Christian era. Every London child up to the time of Shakespeare was taught about those old kings and knew the places associated with them. On Ludgate Hill, named after King Lud who fortified London in about 70 B.C. stood the temple of Apollo on the site now occupied by St. Paul's Cathedral.All around it, in the traditional square-mile area of the city, were numerous shrines. Their sites were presumably located following the invariable practice of antiquity, by the state augurs or geomancers, who professed the art of creating a religious enchantment over cities and countrysides, and their original pattern was largely preserved by the succession of temples and churches built upon the same sites. It survived even the Great Fire of 1666 when Sir Christopher Wren rebuilt most of the old churches on the ruins of their predecessors. Before the fire there were more than a hundred churches, each with its tiny parish, within the city's square mile. In many cases, they have proved to have been located upon the prehistoric sanctuaries.

As London has developed from its ancient foundations, it has constantly received imprints from mystical architects and planners. The influence of masonic augury - a tradition closely guarded and passed down within the fraternity - is apparent in the alignments of medieval churches, such as the Strand line (St. Martin-in-the-Fields; St. Mary-le-Strand; St. Clement Danes; St Dunstan, Fleet Street to Arnold Circus) and the line of five churches, including St. Paul's between St. Clement Danes and St. Dunstan, Stepney. These, no doubt, were planned as part of a larger pattern, whose overall purpose was to attract divine influences and to procure good fortune and prosperity for the citizens of London.

Students of these matters dispute about the duration of the priestly tradition and the degree to which it has persisted in modern times. It is certainly apparent in the 17th and 18th centuries, when some of its principles and methods were applied by learned architects and landscape designers to the creation of miniature paradises in noblemen's estates. An esoteric influence has also been discerned in the works of certain 19th-century church architects. The influence persists to this day, not so much

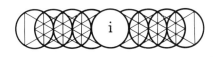

i

through the moribund arcana of masonry as through the autonomous nature of the tradition itself. Being rooted in human nature, through the constant laws of aesthetics which pertain also to the human soul, the tradition is self-renewing.

Every true artist can invoke it and bring its influence to bear on whatever they create. Many in all ages have done so. Chris Street's bold thesis of a sacred design, spanning modern London and extending beyond it, does not, therefore, imply a single human designer. London is the creation of thousands of different builders and architects, working over many centuries. Their common humanity has exposed them to a common influence, and thus together they have created a pattern of which not a single one of them may have been conscious. Chris has discovered that pattern. He has not just dreamt it up, for the fact of its existence is beautifully illustrated on his maps. Yet it is undoubtedly a dream pattern, detached from mundane reality and far transcending both the imagination and the capacity of any town-planning department. In setting out his wondrous discoveries, Chris is exercising the truest and noblest function of a poet, translating images from the world of dreams and ideals into the reality of this present world.

It is impossible to read this honest and visionary book without being deeply affected. The process begins early on , as London's secret pattern is unfolded. The first reaction of the modern educated mind is to be sceptical, even affronted, at this apparent elaboration of nonsense. What are we being asked to believe ? It is soon apparent that no particular beliefs are being asked for. Chris demonstrates his patterns. They are obviously attractive and as we look at them, we fall under a poetic spell.

The critical, rationalizing aspect of our minds is not being challenged or tested. It is simply by-passed and we are immediately engaged on a higher level, through the imagination. On that level the mind is laid open to influence, and here the author takes on a serious responsibility. He could easily , at this stage, have deluded us with personal fantasies. Yet in this book we are not trifled with, for the author is well equal to his responsibility, and under his guidance we follow the classical path through the studies which lead towards initiation.

This journey is naturally delightful, and its pleasures are much enhanced by the charm and intelligence of our guide. He has captured the essence of the ancient tradition. It lives within him and inspires his writing. This is poetry of the the highest quality, serving the highest possible purpose. Here revealed is a world-view, quite different from the low-level, materialistic world-view which dominates modern institutions and evidently destined to replace it.

A transformation of perceptions, both personal and general, seems inevitable in these present times. Chris Street's book is a symptom of that transformation. It is not belittling him to say that it is one of those books that is greater than its human author. It has clearly been written under guidance. To the author's personal credit is that he had made himself worthy of transmitting the insights and revelations which he has invoked directly from the course of an ever-living tradition.

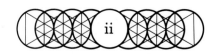

INTRODUCTION

London's outer suburbs contain a number of ancient sacred sites that are of far greater significance than either Westminster Abbey or St. Pauls. To the casual observer, these places don't appear to be anything out of the ordinary, just an assortment of fairly typical parish churches, ancient moats and earthworks, plus the odd beacon hill or ruined abbey. It's not until you realise how they relate to each other geographically that they begin to display an element of the unusual.

They are not scattered about the capital at random. Quite the reverse, in fact. Their positions mark the key points in a network that forms a complex and beautiful geometric pattern covering over 250 square miles around London and radiates out from it to link with numerous other significant sites the length and breadth of the land.

Natural geographical formations have their place in the scheme as well as man-made structures. They fit together in the overall design as neatly as if the English countryside has been landscaped with all the care, precision and ease of a railway modeller's layout.

Though some of these sites are many miles apart, the geometry that links them is astonishingly precise, an intriguing combination of perfect pentagrams and hexagrams, symbols which have always possessed immense mystical and religious significance. To add to the enigma, the pattern they create over London is a temple groundplan relating specifically to the new Jerusalem, St. John's Holy City of Revelation.

Understandably, a discovery of this magnitude raises quite a few important questions. Is the pattern a natural phenomenon, or was it put there by design ? If the sites were laid out to a pre-conceived plan, when was it originated, what was its purpose and who on earth was behind it ? More important, is this the fulfillment of biblical prophesy and is the end nigh ?

The extremely cynical and those who have read some of Von Daniken's early books will be relieved to learn at this early stage in the proceedings that landscape gardeners from outer space do not loom large in any of my answers. As far as I am aware, this is not the handiwork of a flying saucer full of little green Capability Browns. Nevertheless, the explanations and conclusions to be found in later chapters may strike some of you as equally far fetched, if not more so.

This is an enigma on a par with the Great Pyramid or Stonehenge, both of which, incidentally, are founded upon geometrical designs directly related to London's. In common with these two monuments, the places that define this vast example of landscape geometry are ancient sacred sites. As such, their origins are fundamentally linked to humanity's earliest spiritual beliefs, religious practices, customs and rituals - matters which even today do not lend themselves readily to scientific investigation and analysis. Their nature is often more easily grasped intuitively, by the mystic, the psychic, the spiritually sensitive.

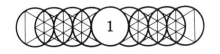

For myself, this particular discovery has definitely had more in common with a spiritual quest than a scientific investigation. It began back in 1976 when I first visited Stonehenge. At that time, tourists were still allowed to mill around the stones and plenty of them were wandering about, festooned with cameras, speculating about the place's raison d'etre.

I don't know why, but it occurred to me that its entire history might actually be preserved and recorded in the stones themselves - or in the atmosphere of the site. I thought that if I could somehow tune into it psychically, some of this otherwise inaccessible information might seep through into my own consciousness. I knew very little about meditation at the time, so I just sat down on the grass and tried to relax into a receptive frame of mind. After fifteen minutes or so, nothing much had happened, except that I'd nearly fallen asleep. Nevertheless, my curiosity regarding the origins and purpose of our ancient sacred sites had been aroused and when I began working with my local sites a few years later, my approach incorporated a lot of what might be called psychic archaeology. Much to my surprise, it actually seemed to work. Not every time, I admit; and not everywhere. The best results occurred when it happened spontaneously, most notably at the sites featured in this book.

Hardly the scientific method, I have to admit, but broadly speaking, that's how this discovery came about. I make no apologies for the shortcomings of the approach. Whatever its faults, it does have certain advantages over other lines of enquiry and those with an open mind and a philosophical attitude will find, as I did, that it lends a completely new perspective to our understanding of the nature and purpose of the Earth's sacred sites, the forces that work through them and humanity's connections to them via our psycho-spiritual dimensions. It allows the currently fragmented knowledge on these subjects to be synthesised into something akin to a coherent whole - and one which is entirely relevant to the emerging spirit of the new age.

This discovery has had a profound effect on me, as St. John's vision of the Holy City doubtless had on him. As with St. John's vision, the old Earth, or at least my former view of it, has passed away and "is no more". It has been replaced with a fuller understanding of humanity's role here on Earth and our place in the universe at large.

For me the world has already changed; the new age begun.

Now it's your turn.

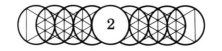

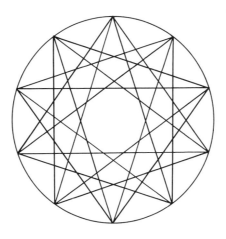

CHAPTER ONE:

STARS IN THE EARTH.

Every geometrical construction develops from a single point and the patterns of this network were no exception to the rule. They grew out of my curiosity for a single site in north London, a place whose name alone singles it out as the ideal spot to begin a spiritual quest. It's called Camelot.

Outside the realms of mythology it exists, not as a mediaeval fortress or fairytale castle, but as a small, secluded moat surrounded by woodland a few miles north of London, near Cockfosters. Over the centuries, its name has been abbreviated to Camlet Moat, but a browse through the local history section of the reference library in nearby Barnet can confirm that in the twelfth century at least, it was definitely known as Camelot. At that time, it was in use as the manor house of Geoffrey de Mandeville, one of our Norman conquerors, Earl of Essex and founder of the Benedictine Monastery of Waldron, a site now occupied by Audley End House, Saffron Waldron.

As a homestead moat, Camlet may actually have been in existence since Saxon times, but whether it was ever home to King Arthur is a matter for pure conjecture. Known records of the place do not penetrate the past far enough to throw any light whatsoever on the matter.

Curiously though, the area does have some other odd Arthurian associations which increased my interest in the site and led me to believe that the place definitely held the keys to some kind of mystery and not necessarily just the one I have unravelled here. Only a couple of miles away at Forty Hall in Enfield, workmen dredging the sludge from a pond discovered a lead cross which to all intents and purposes appeared to be identical to the one which is said to have graced King Arthur's tomb in Glastonbury. Its whereabouts are currently something of a mystery in themselves since its finder, a Mr. Mahoney, promptly hid it elsewhere in the vicinity and elected to spend eighteen months in prison rather than hand it over the local authorities.

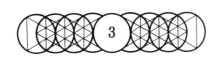

The second Arthurian connection concerns Camlet moat directly and crops up in Gareth Knight's book, *The Secret Tradition in Arthurian Legend*. The book contains a map drawn by the poet, novelist and occultist Charles Williams, clearly showing Camelot in the general area of north London, several hundred miles from Tintagel or Cadbury Castle, the usual candidates for its location. Mr. Williams obviously had good reasons for this, but unfortunately, whatever they were, he seems to have kept them to himself, although one consideration to be born in mind is that he was a member of an occult group called the Society of The Golden Dawn, so we can reasonably assume that he may have been privy to quite a lot of information that could hardly be described as common knowledge.

These findings only served to arouse my curiosity about Camlet Moat even further and in my attempts to delve into its history, I discovered that it had very definite connections with two other ancient sites in the vicinity.

One of them is the parish church of St. Mary the Virgin at nearby Monken Hadley. Back in the twelfth century both places were owned by Geoffrey de Mandeville, although the site St. Mary's now occupies was not originally a church. It was an establishment called the Hermitage at Hadley and in those days, a hermit was often a lone follower of the Hermetic Tradition, an esoteric teaching system from which orders such as The Golden Dawn were derived. For reasons best known to himself, Geoffrey handed the Hermitage over to the Benedictine monks of Waldron Abbey in 1136 and their chapel may have made way for the first parish church which was built here in 1494.

The connection between the two sites is still present physically in the form of Camlet Way, a road which commences to the rear of the churchyard and is so named because it once led from St. Mary's to Camlet moat, obviously providing direct access to and from Mandeville's Manor. Again, as a site St. Mary's is unique, reputedly the only surviving church in England with a cresset (a beacon burner) atop its tower. The discovery that it had been rebuilt in 1848 by an architect named G.E.Street was an odd coincidence which only served to confirm, in my mind at least, that I should regard it as a place of some personal importance.

The third site lies a couple of miles further south. It's the parish church of St. Mary The Virgin, East Barnet, another church dedicated to St. Mary and founded by Benedictines. When it was built by the monks of St. Alban's Abbey in 1086, it was said to be the only church between London and St. Albans. The fact that it had also been the only church in existence at the time when Camlet Moat provided a manorial residence for Geoffrey de Mandeville persuaded me that it may be of some significance, too. I was convinced that these three sites had other, hidden connections, but at the time, I had very little idea what they might be. The first tangible clue came as a result of an investigation into their potential as mark points on ley-lines. For anyone who has never heard of the term, a ley-line or ley is a perfectly straight alignment of four or more ancient sites or mark-points like standing stones, pre-reformation churches, tumuli, etc, sometimes stretching for miles across the landscape. A Herefordshire businessman

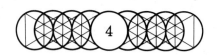

and magistrate, Alfred Watkins, is popularly credited with their discovery around 1920 and they have been a constant cause of controversy ever since. Archaeologists generally refuse to accept that they exist at all, whilst dowsers maintain that enigmatic Earth energies are present at the sites and flow along the alignments between them. However, you can easily settle the question of their existence for yourself by picking up an Ordnance Survey map, pencil and ruler and becoming an armchair ley-hunter.

Fully equipped in this capacity, I checked out the possible alignments through the three locations. At first, it looked a bit of a red herring. The line from Camlet Moat to St. Mary's Monken Hadley didn't extend to any remarkable sites in either direction except one small church just to the north of Enfield. The line from the moat to St. Mary's East Barnet wasn't much more promising. It extended to St. James' Church, Friern Barnet before seemingly petering out.

When I tried an alignment from St. Mary's Monken Hadley to St. Mary's East Barnet however, I found something I hadn't been looking for. The three sites formed a perfectly equilateral triangle (Fig I).

I have to admit that, in isolation, the Barnet triangle doesn't obviously warrant much more than a second thought. After all, any three ancient sites form a triangle and quite a few may even turn out to be equilateral. Nor, to the best of my knowledge, does it draw attention to itself by swallowing assorted aircraft and ships wholesale like the more notorious Bermuda triangle.

Despite this, I was convinced that I had stumbled upon the first piece in a very unusual puzzle, a notion borne out by later developments which revealed the Barnet triangle's role as the key to a far greater geometric pattern of enormous complexity, covering the whole of London and with every indication of extending into a grid system that may not only be national, but global.

Cockfosters' version of Camelot isn't the only surprise lurking in the London suburbs, either. Norbury has something just as impressive, a hill-top henge hidden away amid an estate of neat Edwardian semi-detached houses. It's called Pollard's Hill and although it doesn't so far seem to have been officially recognised as an ancient monument, anyone with a keen eye for such things would immediately suspect that it might be. It's a roughly circular earthwork of irregular banks with a prominent mound at its highest and most northerly point. It may even have contained a stone circle at sometime in its history. In well populated areas these monuments did tend to have their stones removed and broken up to provide homes rather than temples. Sadly, the only structure it now contains is a hideous concrete shelter that provides an unofficial gallery for the work of local graffiti artists.

I stumbled upon Pollard's Hill apparently quite by chance when a friend who knew of my interest in ley-lines, dowsing and Earth energies asked me to check whether I could find any alignments that passed through a building in Great Portland Street that she was interested in. On consulting my maps, the only one which sprang to my attention seemed to

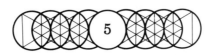

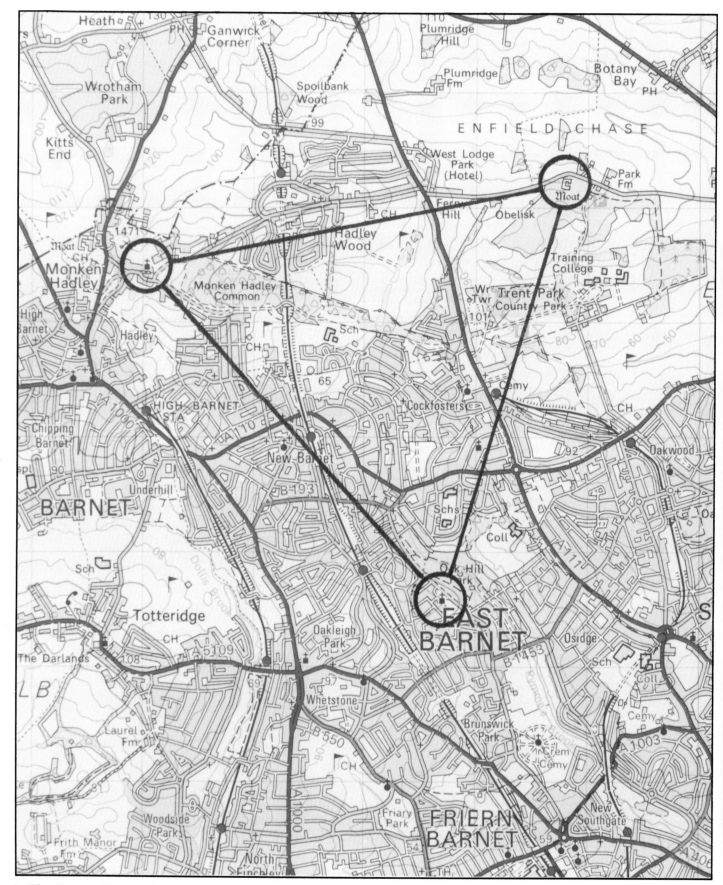

1; The Barnet Triangle :   © Crown copyright

A perfect equilateral triangle on the Hertfordshire landscape formed by three of the area's oldest sites, each of them in some way unique and all directly connected with the Benedictine Order; Camlet Moat in Trent Park, Cockfosters; The parish church of St. Mary the Virgin, Monken Hadley and the parish church of St. Mary the Virgin, East Barnet

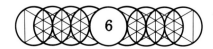

2: The parish church of St. Mary the Virgin, East Barnet.

3: Pollard's Hill, London's hill top henge.

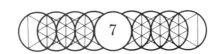

4: The alignment between St. Mary's East Barnet and Pollard's Hill.

Some points of interest that this alignment passes through are: St. Mary's East Barnet; Halliwick Hospital, Friern Barnet; Muswell Hill; The Pavilion in Highgate Woods; St. Joseph's at the summit of Highate Hill; Pond Square, Highgate Hill; The United Reform Church, South Grove, Highgate; The Catacombs in Highgate Cemetary; Highgate Baptist Chapel at the Corner of Chetwynd Rd, NW5; The Church of the Holy Trinity, Clarence Way, NWI; Our Lady of the Halo, Arlington Rd, Camden; St. Mary Magdalene, Munster Square, NWI; The Central Synagogue, Hallam St. WI; The Queen Victoria Memorial Fountain in front of Buckingham Palace; Westminster Cathedral; The Church of St. George and St. Andrew, Patmore St, Nine Elms; St. Peter's Parish Church, Clapham Manor Rd; St. Leonard's Parish Church, Streatham; The Church of Immanuel with St. Anselm, Streatham Common; St. Bartholemew's Catholic Church, South Streatham; Pollard's Hill, Norbury.

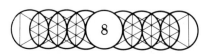

begin at St. Mary's East Barnet and could be tracked right across London to a very interesting-looking, hill-top site which, judging by the symbols on the OS map, commanded panoramic views over the surrounding area and was utilised as an Ordnance Survey triangulation point. It turned out to be Pollard's Hill.

Since the alignment itself (Fig 4) passed through quite a few possible ley mark-points, I immediately felt that it was somehow relevant and that Pollard's Hill was another significant piece of the puzzle, although where it fitted into the overall scheme of things was not immediately apparent.

After several unsuccessful attempts to find any other noteworthy connections between Pollard's Hill and the three points of the Barnet triangle, I stumbled upon the fact that there was a possible triangular relationship between the hill and two churches in the vicinity. The triangle they formed wasn't perfectly equilateral like Barnet's and of the two sites, only one, St. Mary's Beddington, had a lengthy history. A place of worship was recorded here in the Doomsday Book and it is believed that a church has stood on the spot since Saxon times, an opinion supported by archaeological finds indicating the presence of an Anglo-Saxon burial ground nearby. By comparison, the second site, St. Mary's Addiscombe, is a relatively new addition to the area, being a fairly typical example of Victorian Gothic. Nevertheless, I marked the Croydon triangle on the map as a possible clue for future reference (Fig 5).

Sometime later, it struck me that the two triangles were roughly equidistant from central London and that if the line between them was taken as a diameter, the circle so created would enclose almost all of London. I decided to see if there were any other interesting sites it might draw to my attention.

The central point turned out to be slightly north of Oxford Circus mid-way between the Central Synagogue, Hallam Street and All Souls, Langham Place. I took a radius to St. Mary's East Barnet and marked the circle upon my map, noting as I did that its circumference passed through an impressive number of churches as well as a several other noteworthy spots, like Horsenden Hill, Harrow, and Caesar's Camp, Wimbledon. Encouraged by this result, I then drew a second circle, radius to Camlet Moat, and was pleased to find that at the southern end of its sweep, it passed directly through one of the sites of the Croydon Triangle, St. Mary's Beddington, thus justifying its inclusion as a relevant part of the pattern.

On closer investigation, I was even more surprised to find that the angle between St. Mary's East Barnet and Horsenden Hill on the inner circle was exactly 72 degrees, with a further 72 degrees marking the angle to Caesar's Camp. I recognised immediately that these three sites marked exact fifth divisions of the circle and so might share a pentagonal relationship. When I calculated the position of the other two pentagonal points, I discovered that they also fell on unusual places. One was St. Gabriel's Church, Wanstead, while the last point was almost on top of the curiously hexagonal Bellingham Green, which boasts a number of mysterious mounds and is overlooked by no less than two churches. The plot had thickened considerably.

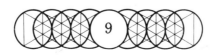

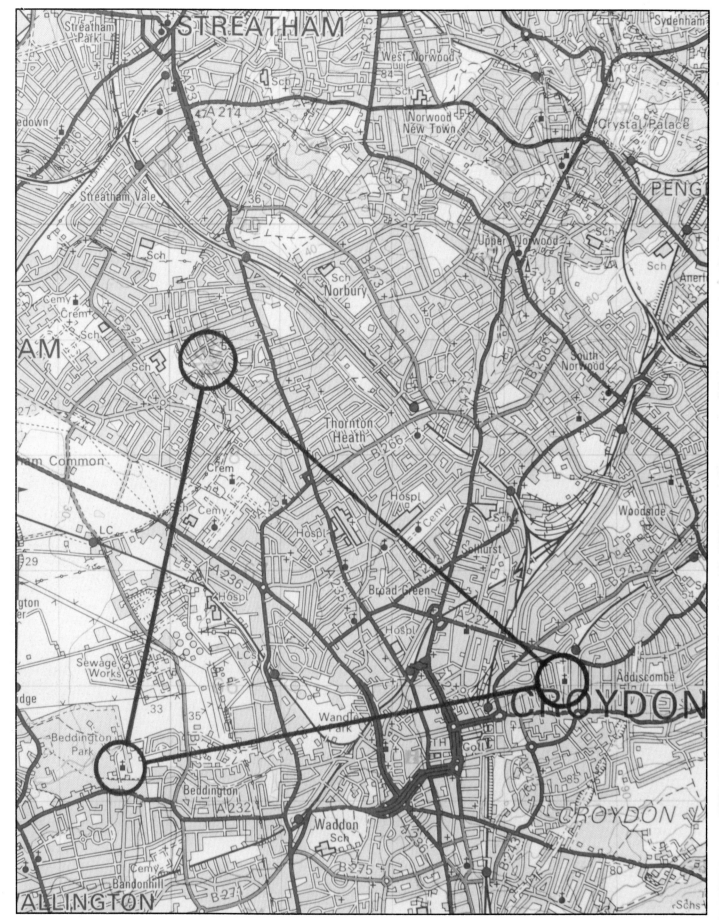

5: The Croydon Triangle.
Pollard's Hill, The parish churches of St. Mary's, Beddington and St. Mary's, Addiscombe.

© Crown copyright

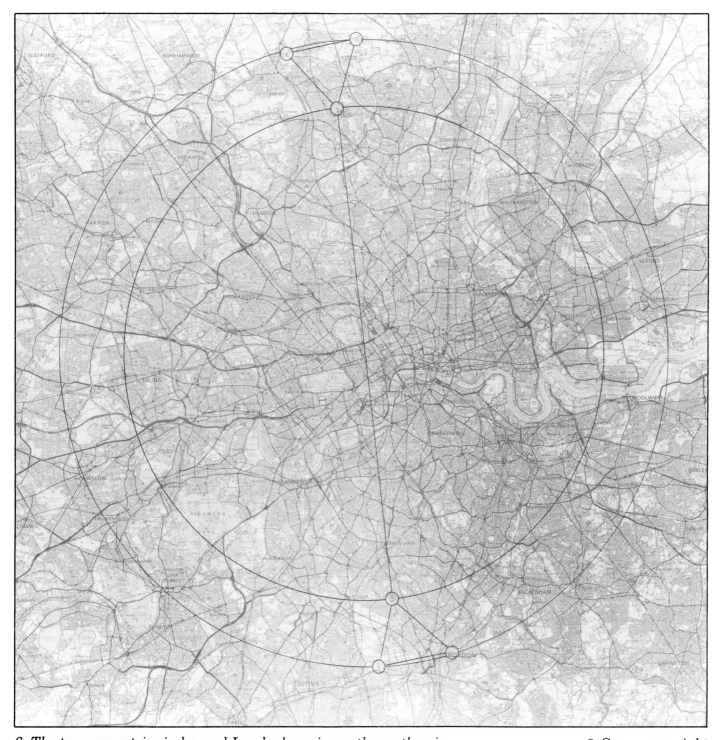

*6: **The two concentric circles and London's main north- south axis.*** © *Crown copyright*

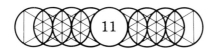

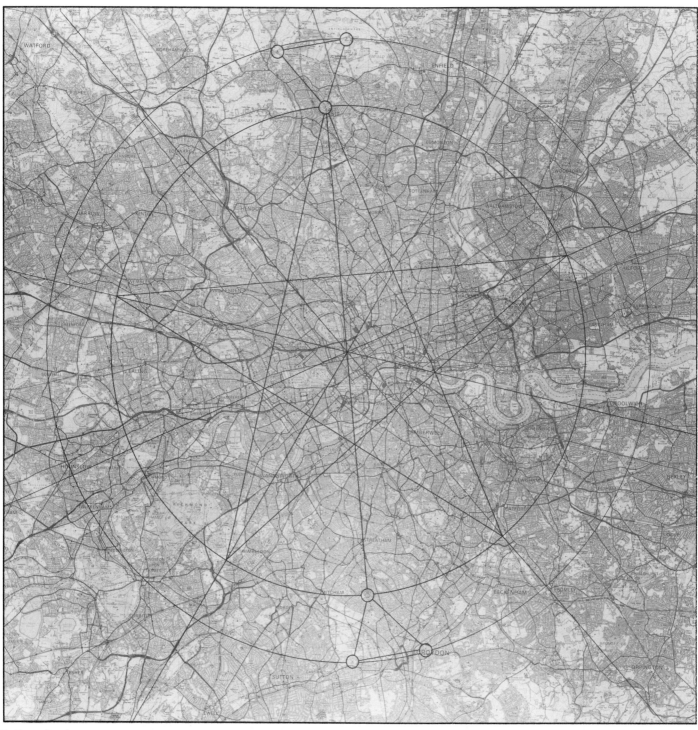

7: London's pentagram: © Crown copyright
Going clockwise from the top, the points are:
1: The parish church of St. Mary The Virgin, East Barnet. 2; The parish church of St. Gabriel, Wanstead. 3;
A point close to Bellingham Green. 4; A point in woodland near Caesar's Camp, Wimbledon. 5; Horsenden Hill,
  Harrow.

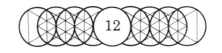

The points of the pentagonal star weren't its only well-defined features, either. The intersections of its constructional lines also hit a few high spots; the most obvious being Tower Hill, one of London's oldest druidic meeting places. Two of the others are churches, one at the junction of West End Lane and Finchley Road, Hampstead, the second, the Church of St. George and St. Andrew in Patmore Street, Nine Elms. The remaining two points are in Highbury Hill and Holland Park.

The alignment through Horsendon Hill and the centre of the pentagram deserves a mention as well. It boasts a spectacular succession of mark sites including Bulstrode Camp Gerrard's Cross, St. James Church, Gerrard's Cross, St Mary's Denham, St Giles Ickenham, Dabb's Hill, St. Barnabas Northolt, Horsenden Hill and Harlesdon Parish Church. In central London it passes through St. Dunstan's and St Bride's in Fleet Street, then wings onwards to Tower Hill and beyond.

For the pentagram to include such an impressive alignment was convincing evidence that I was not creating a mare's nest on the map. From that moment on, I concentrated on looking for star patterns rather than simple straight alignments and I was not to be disappointed. The two triangles which had previously yielded nothing spectacular in the way of straight lines turned up trumps when extended to different points on the circumference of the circles.

The structures of the two triangles at Barnet and Croydon exert a controlling influence over far more complex patterns within the capital's two concentric circles. Every line of each triangle generates a different geometric figure, all of them related in such a way that the seemingly simple geometry of the two initiating triangles has to be assessed anew as a work of such precision and complexity that it is nothing short of miraculous.

For example, the line from St. Mary's Monken Hadley to St. Mary's East Barnet enters the circle at an angle of 36 degrees to the radius and strikes the circumference at an angle of 108 degrees to its point of entry. This is not just any old line across a circle. It creates an arc that is precisely three tenths of the circle's circumference and if continued around the circle at the same angulation (72 degrees), it would eventually define all ten points of a star decagram (Fig 8). The fact that five of those points were already marked by the previous pentagram would seem to indicate that this is not the result of coincidence or chance. They are clearly both a part of the same overall design.

The line from Camlet Moat to St. Mary's East Barnet adds a third figure, yet at the same time provides additional evidence that they are all intrinsic parts of the same vast pattern. It enters the circle at an angle of 22.5 degrees to the radius and extends across it to mark a point at 135 degrees to St. Mary's East Barnet.

This just happens to define a precise eighth division of the circle and so again is not a random line. It is a line between two points of an octogon. In fact, the figure of a complete eight-pointed star may be constructed by simply repeating the previously described process of extending the line

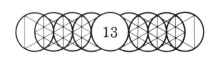

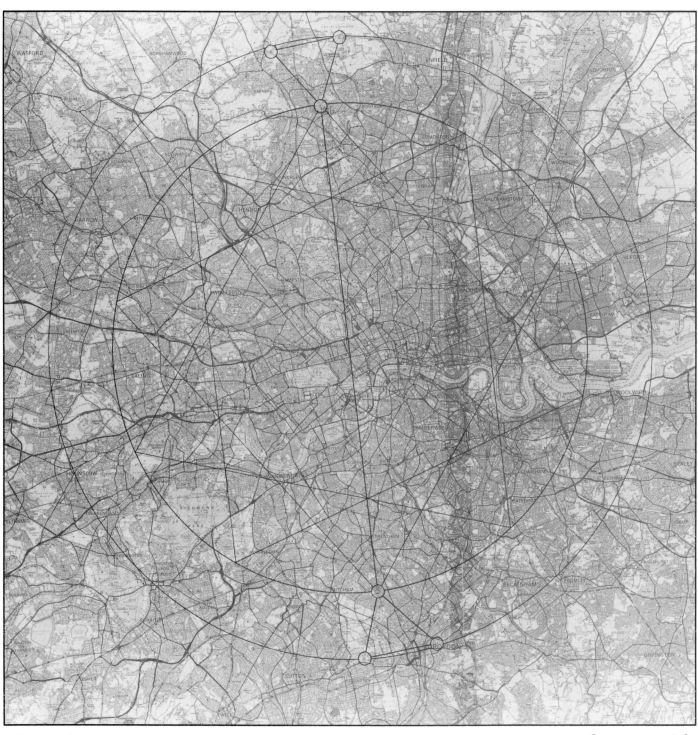

8: London's star decagram,   © Crown copyright

formed by an extension of the alignment from St Mary's Monken Hadley to St. Mary's East Barnet. Points clockwise are: 1; St. Mary's East Barnet. 2: Lea Valley Park, Enfield. 3; St. Gabriel's, Wanstead. 4; St. Catherine's Catholic Church, Charlton. 5; Bellingham Green. 6; Pollard's Hill, Norbury. 7; Caesar's Camp, Wimbledon. 8; Sion Park, Brentford, originally the site of a Brigetine Priory. 9; Horsenden Hill, Harrow. 10: Watling Park, Burnt Oak.

around the inner circumference of the circle, repeating its angulation. Eventually, it hits all eight points precisely (Fig 9).

By now, I was beginning to get curious about what the third side of the triangle might generate on the outer circle. It proved to be an even bigger surprise, an eighteen-sided polyhedron (Fig 10). Extended from Camlet Moat through St. Mary's Monken Hadley, it strikes the circle at an angle of 80 degrees and can be deflected around the inside perimeter at 160 degrees to make eighteen perfectly spaced contacts with the circumference.

To finally dispel any doubt about the validity of the Croydon triangle's inclusion in the design, its sides generate several more figures, all of which fit perfectly into the plan so far formed. The first is the same eighteen sided polyhedron, previously produced from the Barnet triangle. The base of the Croydon triangle, the line between St. Mary's Beddington and St. Mary's Addiscombe forms precisely the same pattern.

In addition, the alignment from St. Mary's Beddington to Pollard's Hill creates an inverted pentagram on the inner circle (Fig 11). Apart from sharing the same axes and five points of the decagram, it is a mirror image of the first inner circle pentagram. They are an interlocking matched pair, designed to function together as a perfectly balanced set of opposites.

Similar patterns can be found when we turn our attention to the east and west points, despite the fact that neither of the two appear to be directly located on any building or natural feature of special interest. The closest sites of any significance are Kensington Cemetery in Hanwell, west London and The Elim Church in Central Park Rd, on the eastern side. Nevertheless, in both cases, there are two extremely important sacred sites in each area which complete an interesting triangular relationship comparable to those at Barnet and Croydon.

The East Ham triangle (Fig 12) is defined by the eastern point of the circle, Barking Abbey which was founded in 666 AD. and St. Mary Magdalene, the parish church of East Ham, built in 1130 and, according to the guide book, the only Norman church in London to have survived intact.

The Hanwell triangle (Fig 13) stems from the relationship between the western point of the circle, St. Mary's Hanwell and St. Mary's Norwood Green, yet another church dating back to Norman times.

At first, I was a little disappointed that neither the east nor west triangle was equilateral, isosceles or in any other way individually remarkable. In fact, they're both quite odd little shapes and, like the Barnet and Croydon triangles, almost mirror images of each other.

The patterns they generate though are quite startling, both in themselves and in the impressive way they combine with those already produced by the triangles at Barnet and Croydon.

The East Ham and Hanwell triangles both give rise to pentagrams within the inner circle and like the triangles that generate them, they are a perfectly matched pair of mirror images, interconnecting with each other via their shared axes to form a composite ten-pointed star (Figs 14 & 15).

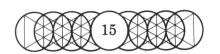

15

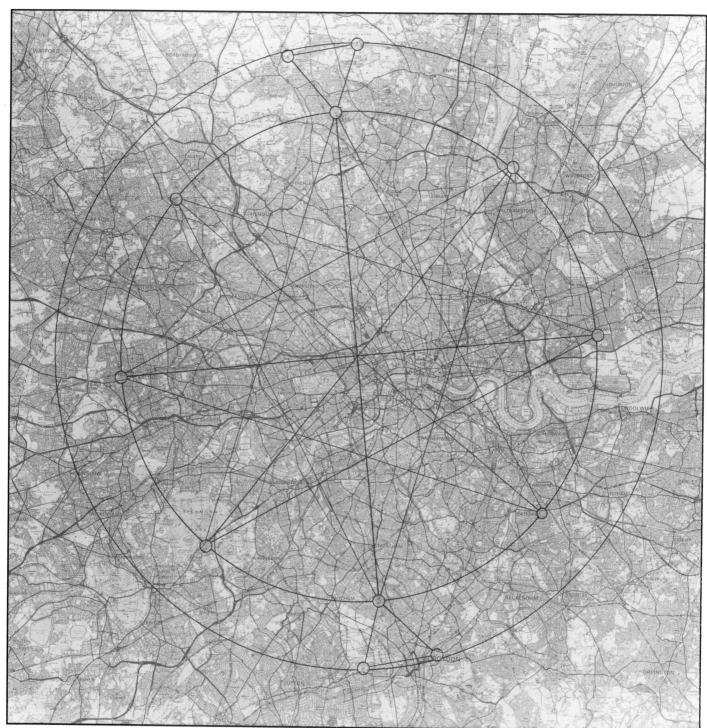

9: The eight-pointed star;

formed by an extension of the alignment from Camlet Moat to St. Mary's East Barnet. Points in clockwise rotation: 1; St. Mary's East Barnet. 2; Playing fields adjacent to Chingford Rd, Enfield. 3; The eastern point of the circle, near Central Park, East Ham. 4: Hither Green Methodist Church, Torridon Road, S.E.6. 5; Pollard's Hill, Norbury. 6; A point near Ulleswater Crescent, Kingston Vale. 7; The western point of the circle, Kensington Cemetery, Hanwell. 8; A point on the wide, grassy central reservation, Station Parade, Queensbury.

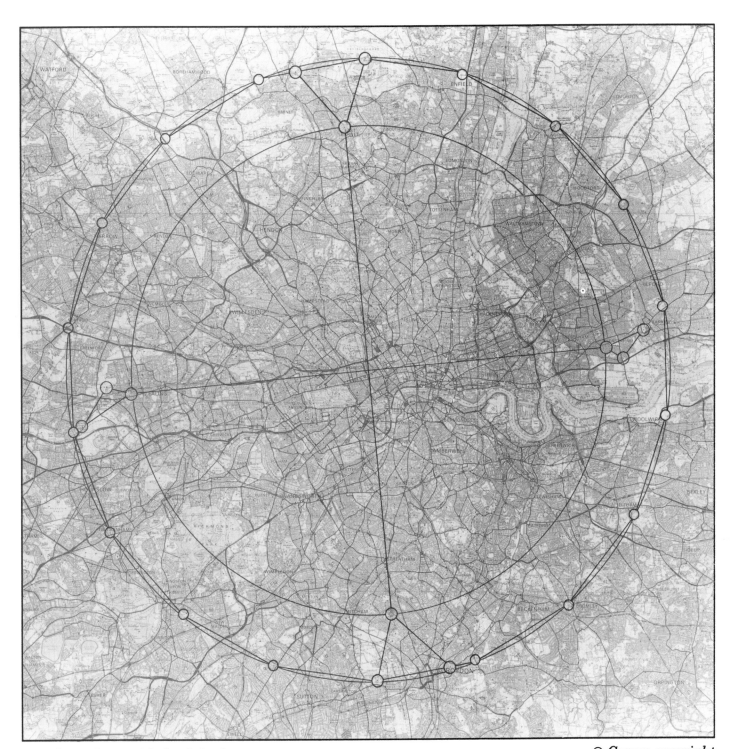

10: The eighteen-sided polyhedron   © Crown copyright

formed by the extension of the line from Camlet Moat to St. Mary's Monken Hadley. Points in clockwise rotation: 1; Camlet Moat. 2; Enfield playing fields near the Queen Elizabeth Stadium's Pavilion. 3; Hilltop point in Station Road, Chingford. 4; Small wood bordering parkland near Heathcote Avenue, Clayhill. 5; Point in Highfields Road, Woodford Green. 6; Recreation ground near Plumstead Marsh. 7; Grounds of Charlton Park RFC, behind the Parish Church of The Holy Trinity, Eltham. 8; St. Martin's Hill Park, Bromley, on top of the hill near the war memorial. 9; The Catholic Church of Our Lady of The Annunciation, Bingham Road, Addiscombe. 10; The Parish Church of St. Mary The Virgin, Beddington. 11; St. Anthony's Hospital on the A 24. 12; The chapel of Kingston Cemetery, Norbiton. 13; A point close to The Parish Church of All Saints, Twickenham. 14; Central reservation of The Glen at the Cranewater Park end, Norwood Green. 15; Northolt Methodist Church at the corner of the A40 and A312. 16; Corner of Harrow View and Headstone Gardens. 17; Point in fields east of the A41 near Elstree (On the OS map a spring is indicated in the immediate vicinity). 18; Open field to the west of Galley Lane, Arkley, Barnet.

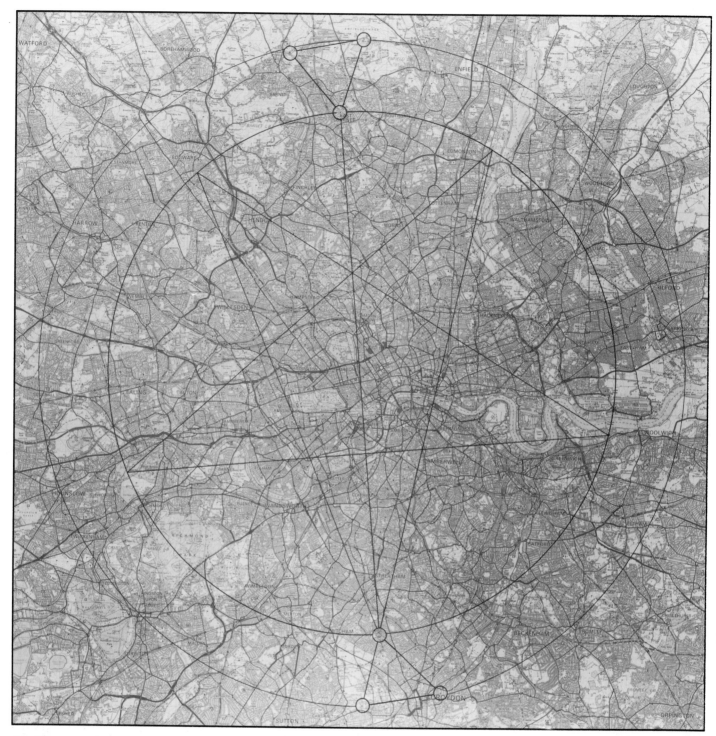

11: The pentagram generated by the Croydon triangle.
It interconnects perfectly with the pentagram and decagram generated by the Barnet triangle.

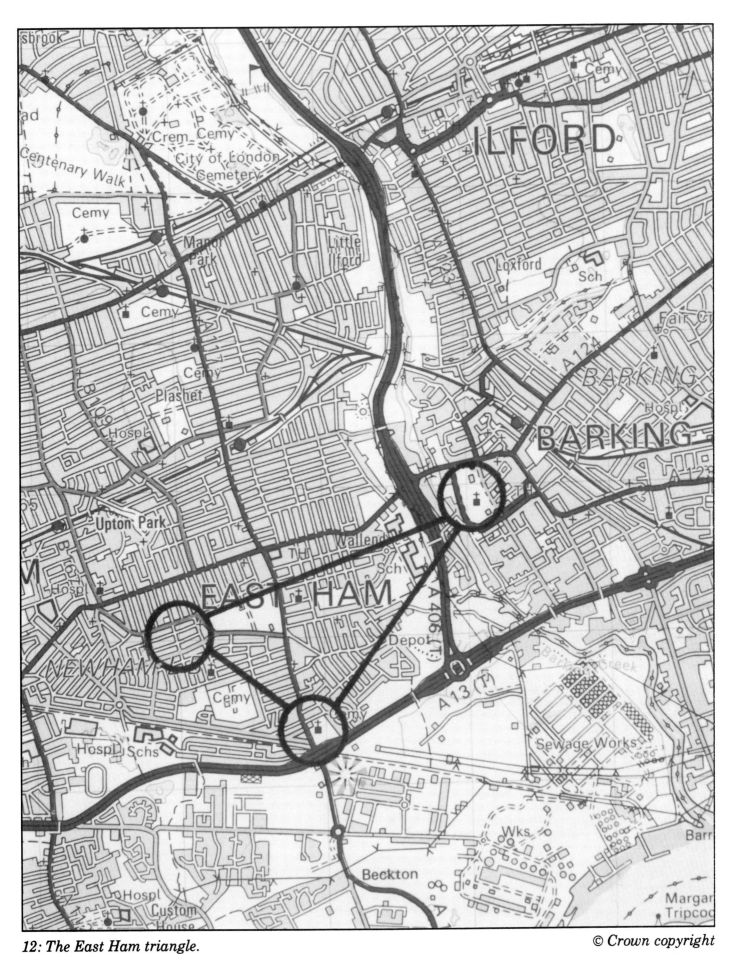

12: The East Ham triangle.   © *Crown copyright*

1: The eastern point of the circle. 2: Barking Abbey, founded in 666 AD and now in ruins. Immediately adjacent is St. Margaret's Church. 3: St. Mary Magdalene, the parish church of East Ham, built in 1130, it is claimed to be the only Norman church in London to have survived intact. It may actually mark an even earlier Roman sacred site as coffins which are now in the British Museum were excavated from a Roman cemetery close by.

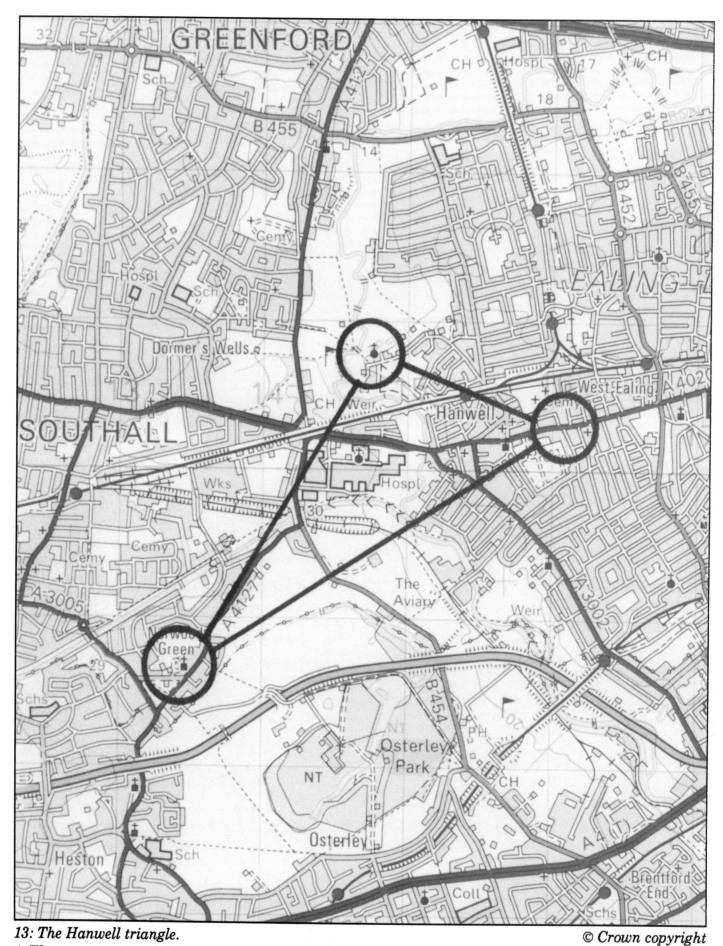

13: The Hanwell triangle.   © *Crown copyright*
1: The western point of the circle. 2: The parish church of St. Mary, Hanwell. The present building dates from 1846, but stands on the site of a much earlier church. 3: St. Mary's Parish Church, Norwood Green, a small church with a known history dating back to Norman times.

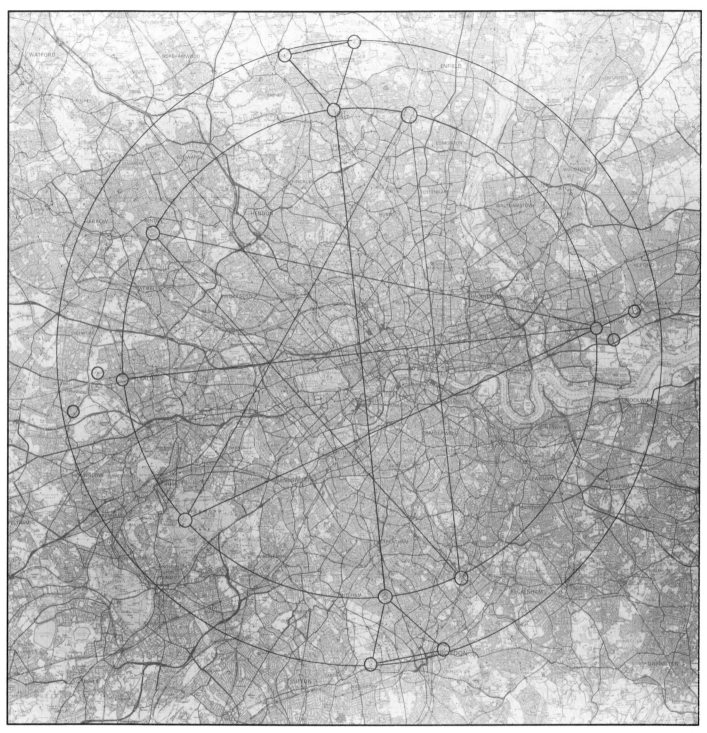

14: The Eastern pentagram: © *Crown copyright*
1: The eastern point of the inner circle. 2: Point in a field near Annerley Town Hall. 3: Point in a wood in
Richmond Park. 4: A local high point in Woodhill Crescent, Kenton. 5: A point near Station Rd,
Winchmore Hill.

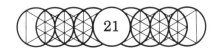

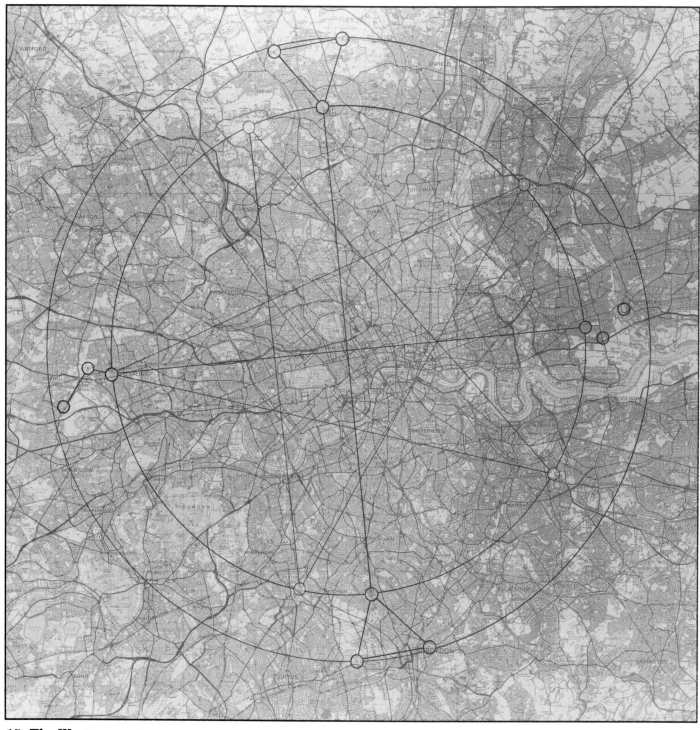

15: The Western pentagram:
1: The western point of the circle. 2: Point on the footpath between Burtonhole Lane and Totteridge. 3: Point in Hale End Rd, E17. 4: Point in Weigall Rd Sports Ground, Eltham. 5: Rock Terrace Recreation Ground, Phipp's Bridge Rd, SW19.

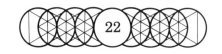

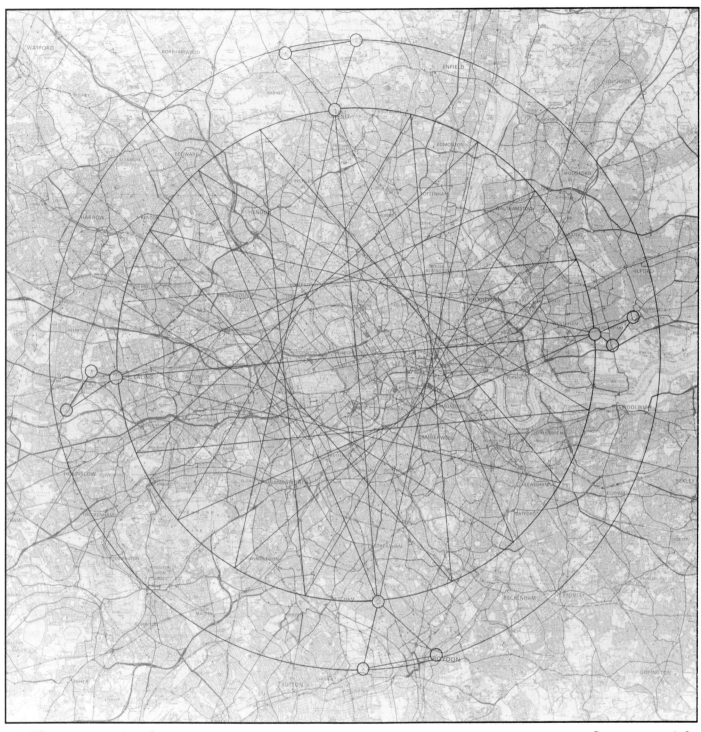

16: The twenty-pointed star,
four pentagrams aligned to the four points of the compass.

© *Crown copyright*

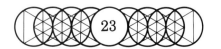

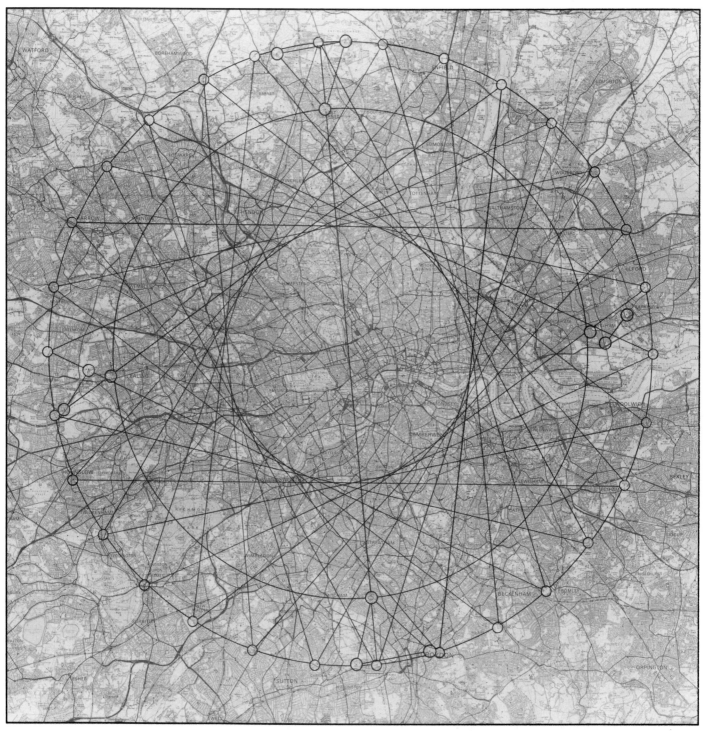

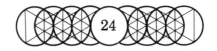

17: The thirty-pointed star.

1: Camlet Way, Hadley Wood. The front garden of a private house. 2: A hilltop site in private gardens near The Ridgeway, Enfield. 3: Near the Queen Elizabeth Stadium in Enfield's playing fields. 4: The middle of King George's Reservoir, Enfield. 5: Field between Brook Road and Whitehall Road, Chingford. 6: Highfield Road, Woodford Bridge. 7: Private Gardens between Otley Drive and Headley Drive, Gant's Hill. 8: Barking Park, near the children's end of the boating lake. 9: The Creekmouth Flood Barrier. 10: Cage Lane Evangelical Free Church. 11: Eltham Warren Golf Course. 12: Court Farm Evangelical Church. 13: St. Martin's Park, Bromley, on top of the hill near the war memorial. 14: Crouch Oak Wood in the grounds of Bethlem Hospital, Eden Park. 15: Ashburton Avenue, Addiscombe. 16, Overgrown wasteland to the east of a large car park, Commerce Way, Waddon. 17: The Wrythe, marked on the map as allotments behind the north side of Wrythe Lane. In fact the land is now overgrown. 18: St. Anthony's Hospital on the A24 in North Cheam. 19: London School of Economics Sports Ground, opposite Balgazette Gardens in Windsor Avenue, Kingston. 20: All Saint's Church, Kingston. There has been a church on this site for well over a thousand years. It's also reputed to be the original location of The King's Stone from which the town derives its name. 21: Strawberry Hill Rd, Twickenham. 22: Whitton Rd, near Hounslow Station. 23: The Glen, Norwood Green. 24: A pond near the Grand Union Canal between Greenford and Southall. 25: A high point at the end of Dabb's Hill Road. Presumably it was once the top of Dabb's Hill, now marked by a small tree in a triangular patch of grass. 26: Somerset Rd, Harrow. 27: Grass central reservation in Woodlands Drive, Stanmore. 28: Point in fields to the east of the A41 near Elstree. 29: The grounds of Saffron Green School, Borehamwood. 30: Field to the north of Barnet Grid Sub-Station, off St. Alban's Rd, Barnet.

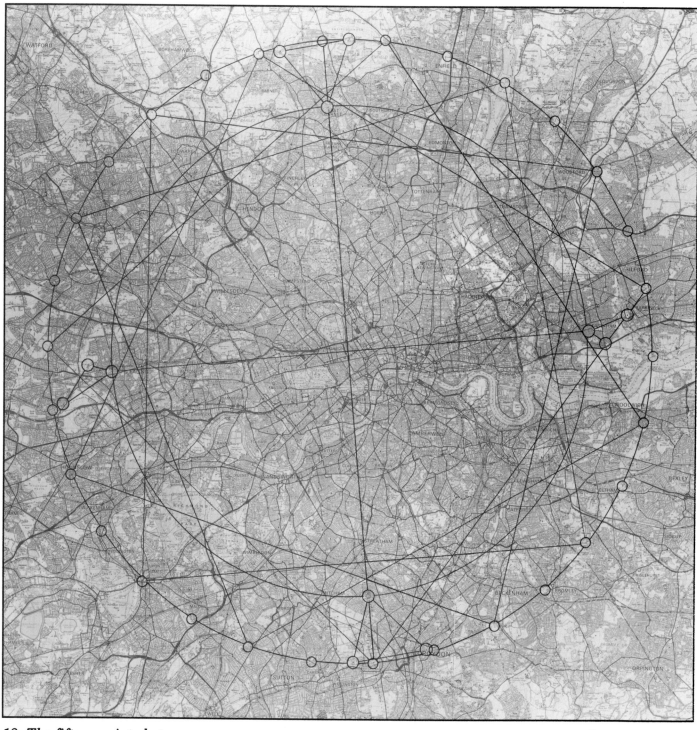

18: The fifteen-pointed star.

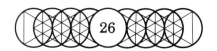

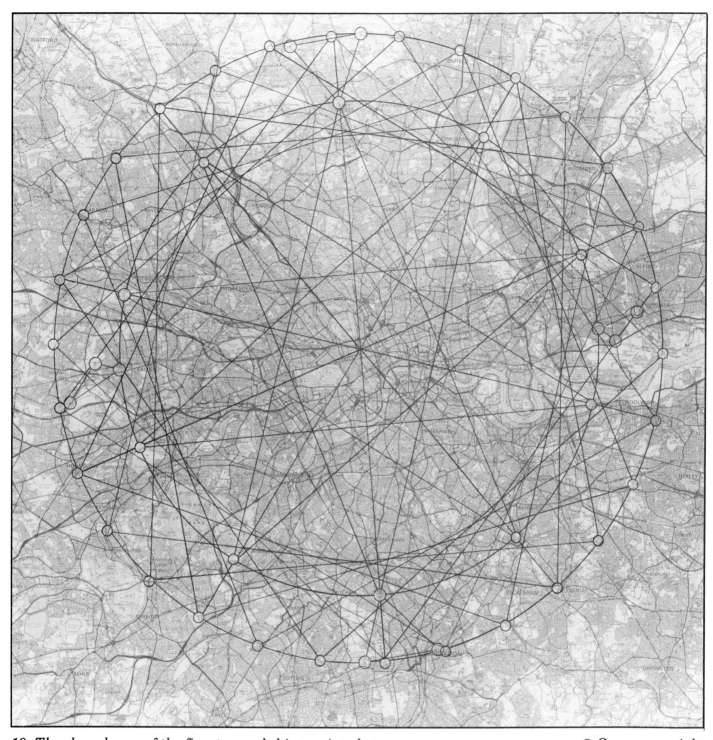

19: The shared axes of the five, ten and thirty-pointed stars.   © *Crown copyright*

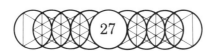

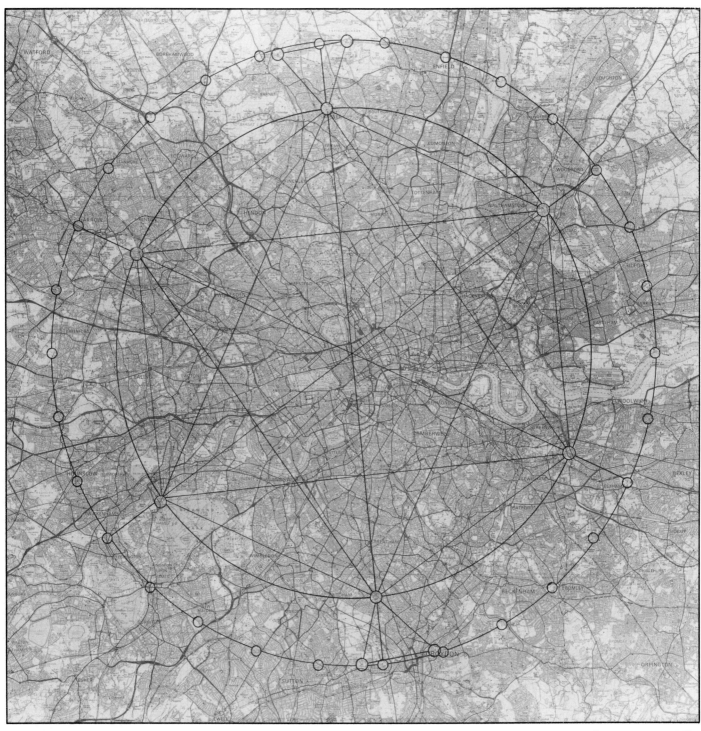

20: The inner circle hexagram. © *Crown copyright*
1: St. Mary's, East Barnet. 2: Point in Epping Forest, Snaresbrook Rd, near Wanstead. 3: St. John Fisher Catholic Church, Kidbrooke. 4: Pollard's Hill, Norbury. 5: Point near the top of Richmond Hill. 6: Grounds of Byron Court Primary School, Kenton.

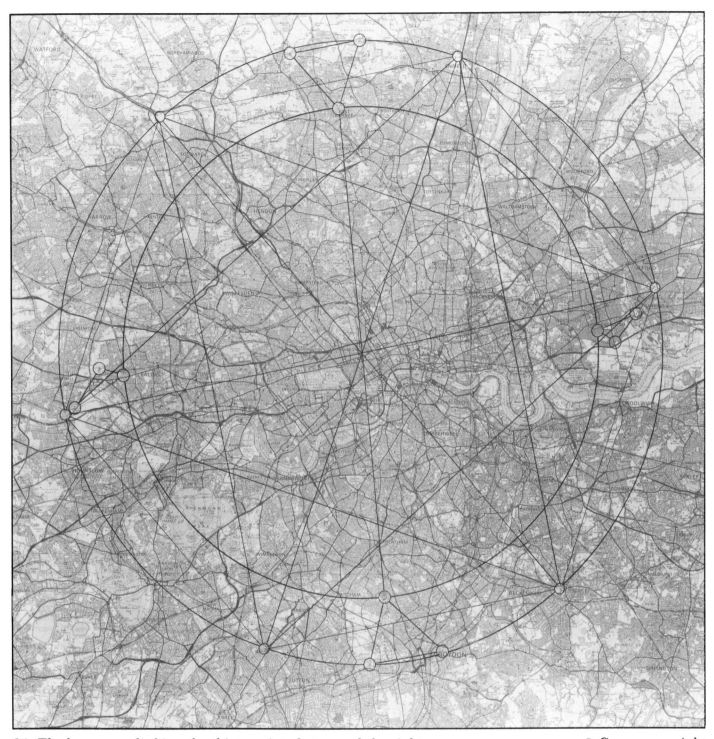

21: *The hexagram linking the thirty-pointed star and the eighteen.*   © *Crown copyright*

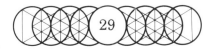

The eastern pentagram is formed by an extension of the line from Barking Abbey to the circle's eastern point. The western pentagram, by an extension of the line from St. Mary's, Hanwell, to the western point of the circle.

As if to emphasise that they too are no random creation, they form an integral part of the existing patterns, combining with them to form a perfect twenty pointed star whose essential construction is based upon four interpenetrating pentagrams, each one aligned to one of the four cardinal points (Fig 16).

An even more complex star pattern can be created from an alignment that originates in the Hanwell triangle. The line from St. Mary's Norwood Green to the western point of the inner circle extends across London to a spot right in the middle of King George's reservoir, Enfield. It creates an angle of 24 degrees to the circle's radius and may therefore be deflected around the circle at an angle of 48 degrees, eventually creating a thirty-pointed star (Fig 17).

Once again, additional confirmation of the figure's validity is provided by an alignment from one of the other triangles. This time, by a line from Barking Abbey through St. Mary's East Ham to the most southerly point of the outer circle. It doesn't actually create the same thirty-pointed star, just half of it, a fifteen-pointed star that utilises every alternate point of the thirty (Fig 18).

As with so many of the previous figures, inherent within the construction of the thirty-pointed star is clear evidence of its relationship to the existing patterns. It shares the same five foundational axes as the Barnet triangle's decagram and the Croydon triangle's inverted pentagram. The radials from the centre to their points on the circumference of the inner circle naturally extend directly to ten of the thirty's points on the outer circle (Fig 19).

However, its remaining axes draw attention to a further geometric pattern which arises from within the overall structure rather than being generated from any external alignment. It is a perfect hexagram defined on the inner circle where six radials of the thirty-pointed star intersect its circumference (Fig 20). It is aligned to the network's north-south axis which is of course defined defined by our two sites of paramount importance, St. Mary's East Barnet and Pollard's Hill.

By now, you're probably getting a little dizzy from seeing all these stars. Stay with it. Only one final figure remains to be revealed, an illustration of the relationship between the thirty pointed star and the eighteen. They share six points in common, all of which are equally spaced at intervals of 60 degrees around the circumference of the outer circle. Another perfect hexagram, curiously angled at 24 degrees to the axis of all the other figures (Fig 21).

Altogether, this brings the grand total of star patterns covering London to twelve, more than enough for a full zodiac. On the outer circle, a hexagram, a fifteen-pointed star, an eighteen and a thirty. On the inner, four pentagrams, a hexagram, an eight, a ten and a twenty.

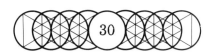

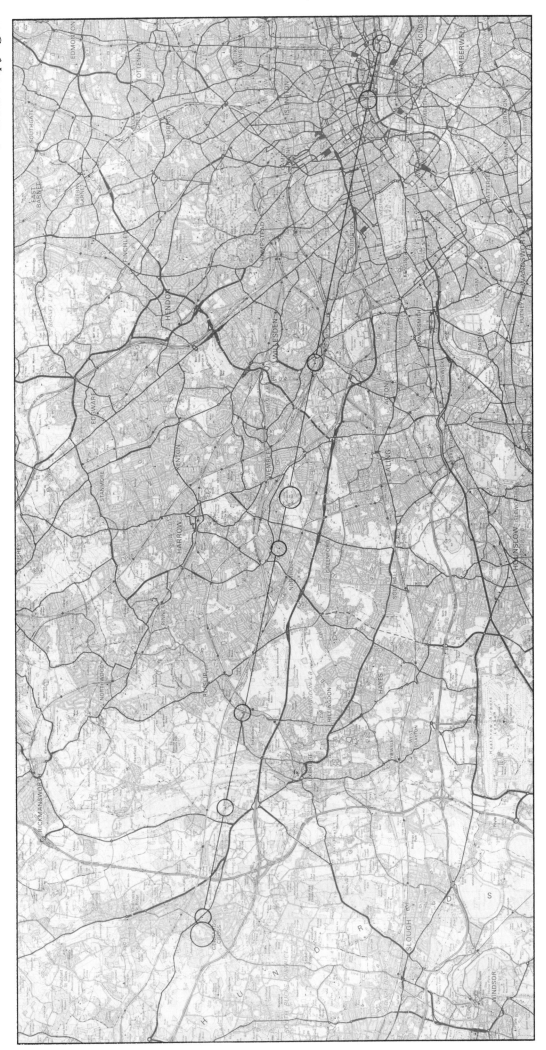

22: The Tower of London - Horsenden Hill Starline. A main axis of the pentagram and decagram. Principal mark points: Bulstrode Camp Gerrard's Cross;
St. James' Church, Gerrard's Cross; St. Mary's Denham; St. Giles Church, Ickenham; The summit of Dabb's Hill; St. Barnabas' Church, Northolt; Horsenden
Hill, Harrow; Harlesdon Parish Church; Central Synagogue, Hallam St, WI; St. Dunstan's, Fleet Street; St. Bride's, Fleet Street; St. Clement's; Tower Hill

By no stretch of the imagination could they be regarded as a freak of nature, a chance occurance. There are too many coincidences to be a coincidence. Despite the fact that all of the individual patterns are generated by four triangles, each at least eight miles apart, they cannot be regarded as isolated figures. They all interconnect so precisely that they can only be interpreted as an integrated whole, a composite design so complex that chance, the easy answer to the non-thinking man's enigma, seems the least likely solution.

The unfailing regularity with which significant places crop up on these alignments only seems to confirm this impression. Within the boundaries of the two circles, many well-known ancient and sacred sites can be found dotted along the lines between the major points. The Tower of London is on one of the shared axes of the five, ten and thirty pointed stars, a line that also passes through Horsenden Hill, Bulstrode Camp and the 6th century site of St. Bride's Fleet Street, as well as parish churches at Ickenham, Denham and Gerrard's Cross (Fig 22).

The summits of Parliament Hill and Primrose Hill both fall on an alignment from St. Mary's East Barnet to point 17 of the star 30. Westminster Abbey, being one of London's most ancient sacred sites, turns out to be a focal point for quite a few alignments. It falls on lines from St. Mary's Addiscombe to St. Mary's Monken Hadley, from point 4 to point 13 of the twenty pointed star, from the Syon House point of the decagon to St. Mary's East Ham, and from the Queensbury point of the eight pointed star to St. Mary's Beddington. St. Paul's Cathedral falls on alignments from Camlet Moat to point 10 of the twenty pointed star, from Pollard's Hill to point 3 of the thirty and point 2 of the eighteen, from the Snaresbrook Road, Epping Forest point of the inner circle hexagram to Caesar's Camp on the pentagram.

Beyond London the alignments continue to link up with similar sites all over the country. The main east-west axis for example, extends to Prittlewell Priory in Southend, via a number of lesser religious houses. To the west, it leads to Silbury Hill, Britain's largest man-made mound and adds a large number of more recent religious constructions to its weight of evidence along the way, finally meeting the Bristol Channel near Brean Down.

The north-south axis also has its share of interesting sites. To the north of London, it passes directly through St. Nicholas's Church at The Bury, Stevenage, a twelfth century establishment with links to the Benedictines of Westminster Abbey and if the etymology of the word bury is anything to go by, a burial ground and sacred site long before the monks arrived. The alignment eventually extends as far as Robin Hood's Bay, near Whitby Abbey on the North Yorkshire coast.

In the opposite direction, it leads laser-like to a striking succession of hilltops, mostly marked with ancient churches like St. John's at Old Coulsden, St. Leonard's at Turner's Hill and St. Peter's at Ardingly. The most southerly point is in Rottingdean, very close to St. Margaret's Church where a place of worship has stood since Saxon times. The precise location here seems to be the village green which boasts an ancient well and several stones which may be the remnants of a megalithic temple. One of the

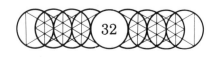

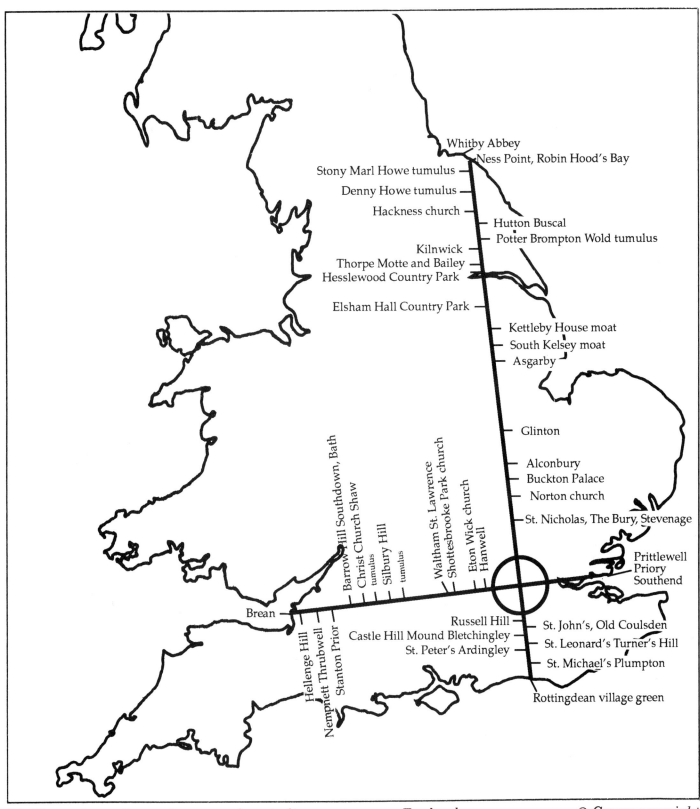

Whitby Abbey
Ness Point, Robin Hood's Bay
Stony Marl Howe tumulus
Denny Howe tumulus
Hackness church
Hutton Buscal
Potter Brompton Wold tumulus
Kilnwick
Thorpe Motte and Bailey
Hesslewood Country Park
Elsham Hall Country Park
Kettleby House moat
South Kelsey moat
Asgarby
Glinton
Alconbury
Buckton Palace
Norton church
St. Nicholas, The Bury, Stevenage
Prittlewell Priory Southend
Barrow Hill Southdown, Bath
Christ Church Shaw
tumulus
Silbury Hill
tumulus
Waltham St. Lawrence
Shottesbrooke Park church
Eton Wick church
Hanwell
Brean
Russell Hill
St. John's, Old Coulsden
Castle Hill Mound Bletchingley
St. Leonard's Turner's Hill
St. Peter's Ardingley
St. Michael's Plumpton
Hellenge Hill
Nempnett Thrubwell
Stanton Prior
Rottingdean village green

23: *The main north, south, east and west alignments across England.*   © Crown copyright

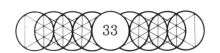

33

stones is still standing, embedded in the road to the west of the green beside North End House.

How the patterns progress into central London as well as how their principal alignments extend from the capital into the surrounding countryside and from there to the rest of the British Isles could fill a very thick volume and probably eventually will. But having already established that stars do exist upon the Earth as well as in the heavens and that they form part of a coherent pattern, there seems little point in presenting you with a lot more maps.

What you need first is some kind of an explanation.

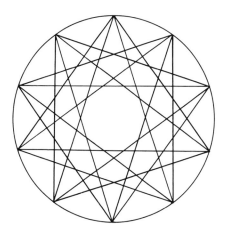

CHAPTER TWO

WHAT THEY DIDN'T TELL YOU ABOUT GEOMETRY AT SCHOOL

The patterns of this network aren't the only geometric designs to be discovered around the English countryside by the keen observer. Throughout nature, a number of basic geometric structures consistently recur as the blueprint for all manner of physical forms, animal, vegetable and mineral. They can be seen in the arrangement of petals on flowers, the arms of starfish, the structure of snowflakes, honeycombs and crystals to name but a few. Wherever it is clearly discernable, life's rich pattern seems to be dominated by the pentagram and the hexagram.

These two geometric forms embody laws of proportion and progression that are also evident, although not quite so overtly, in many of Mother Nature's other creations, including more complex organisms like animals and human beings.

The underlying principle behind the pentagram, the hexagram and a great many other things may be traced back to something Plato called the Golden Mean, a proportional relationship guaranteed to imbue any structure or design with symmetrical perfection since it ensured that every individual part would relate harmoniously, not just to the complete structure as a whole, but to every other part within it.

Researchers have discerned its influence behind the formation of such diverse forms as snails' shells, fir cones, daisy seed heads, animals' skeletons and in the human frame from top to toe, suitable examples here being in the proportions of the facial features and the bones in the feet, not to mention a variety of items in between.

Vitruvius and Fludd's drawings of man superimposed on a pentagram are not a superficial analogy, but an illustration of the fact that both are based upon the same mathematical laws of proportion.

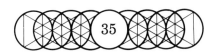

24: *The hexagonal symmetry of a typical snowflake (Science Photo Library)*

25: *A micro-electrograph showing a hexagonal formation of Uranium atoms. (Science Photo Library)*

26: *Pentagonal symmetry common to many flowers.*

27: *A typically pentagonal starfish.*

28: *A pollen grain with an obvious geometric basis. (Science Photo Library)*

29: *The hexagonal structure of a honeycomb.*

The Golden Mean cannot be calculated absolutely. Its most elementary expression is a ratio of 1:1.618033.... however, it can also be expressed numerically as a Fibonacci series, that is a progression which increases by constantly repeating the sum of the last two numbers to create the next. E.g; I, 2, 3, 5, 8, 13, 21, 34, 55, 89, 144, 235, etc. The ratio between any consecutive numbers of a Fibonacci series is always an approximation of the Golden Mean. The inexactitude of its mathematics results from the fact that the Golden Mean derives primarily from a geometric relationship and the figure that best expresses it is none other than the pentagram whose constructional lines all intersect each other in perfect Golden Mean proportions.

That the same few geometric forms and formulae crop up with unfailing regularity as the governing influences behind the growth and physical structure of all manner of things, from molecules and microscopic organisms to the spirals of galactic nebulae, is by no means a recent observation. Thousands of years ago the initiates of the Pythagorean and

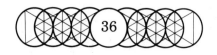

other ancient mystery schools were well aware of these facts. They were taught that the constant recurrence of a few predominant geometric forms and laws throughout the diversity of structures in the natural world was a clear indication that the forces of creation worked along strictly geometric lines.

Their perception of geometry therefore differed enormously from my own dimly recalled memory of it as the ancient art of scraping a blunt pencil and compass across the grubby pages of a school exercise book.

To them, geometry was a sacred science, a study of the divine essence within the mundane and an investigation into the very structure of the universe itself. Geometry's most symmetrical designs were deemed the physical forms through which spiritual force might manifest in the material world. Every point encapsulated the unlimited potential of the universe's creative energy. Every line was a line of divine force. Every angulation represented a modification of that force affecting its nature and purpose, just as the energy of light is modified and broken down into its component elements by the effect of its angulation through a prism. Every geometric pattern was a circuit diagram of how the life-force of the universe functions and is utilised in the material world.

Geometry gave form and definition to the intangible and the infinite, enabling the great minds of the day to more readily comprehend the hidden forces at work within nature and to discern, to some degree at least, the divine plan upon which the whole of creation was built.

From this point of view, a design like the one covering the landscape of London would have to be regarded as a clear manifestation of those forces and therefore not the product of any monumental human effort, but a perfectly natural phenomenon. Its geometric patterns can be understood as a reflection of the inner energies of the planet itself. They would have been present ever since the Earth cooled and solidified from a molten blob of solar plasma, just as a snowflake displays the geometry of its inner structure as it cools and solidifies from a droplet of airborne moisture. If they had a creator at all, it could only be the universal creator, God.

Our remote ancestors must almost certainly have been aware that patterns such as these existed upon the landscape of their world. After all, implicit within the belief that geometric form underlies the fabric of the universe must be an awareness that, as a logical consequence, it must also be the foundation upon which the the physical structure of our planet is built.

Indeed, over two thousand years ago, Socrates hinted somewhat indirectly that the occult structure of the planet was based on a dodecahedron, a geometric solid that exhibits a combination of pentagonal and hexagonal symmetry comparable to London's two-dimensional design. He said that " When viewed from above, the Earth resembles one of those balls which are covered with twelve pieces of leather."

More recently, in the 1960's, Russian scientists echoed his sentiments by putting forward an almost identical theory, suggesting that the Earth's crust is constructed of twelve pentagonal plates which reflect the inner

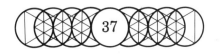

crystalline structure of the planet.

The etymology of the word geometry hints that it has its roots in the Earth, too. It translates literally from the ancient Greek as " the measure of the Earth."

Obviously then, geometry, and in particular the ancient science of sacred geometry, needs looking into in more detail to see if it might shed a little more light on the significance of London's landscape patterns and what precise role they may play as visible expressions of creation's formative forces.

In fact, the design defined by London's sacred sites will be immediately recognisable to scholars of sacred geometry. It is the basis of one of the subject's most significant figures, the culmination of a process known as squaring the circle. Squaring the circle encapsulates the essence of sacred geometry. It is a graphic illustration of how divine force manifests in the mundane world.

The circle is traditionally a symbol of the eternal spiritual realms, the inifinite, the universal and the intangible. It has no beginning, no end and despite being a single, self contained unit, encompasses everything. Any calculation of its dimensions reflects its infinite essence, being based upon the irrational Pi.

The square on the other hand represents the physical world of hard reality, the four corners of the Earth, the four points of the compass, the four seasons, the four alchemical elements of earth, air, fire and water which in turn may be conceived as the four physical states of matter, solid, liquid, gaseous and pure energy. All its dimensions are calculable, finite measures.

Graphically, squaring the circle entails the reconciliation of these two apparent opposites by creating a square equal to a given circle, either in area or circumference.

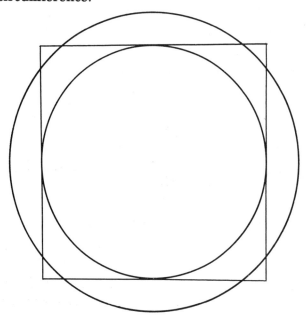

30: The squared circle: The perimeter of the square and circumference of the outer circle are equal.

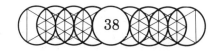

Symbolically, it represents a union between heaven and earth. As a consequence, it was sometimes used as a temple groundplan, to mark a plot of hallowed ground and create a small piece of heaven on Earth.

That London's landscape geometry is based upon identical foundations to the squared circle is undeniable. The proportions of their concentric circles are identical and in sacred geometry, proportion rather than scale is the more important factor. London's two circles are 16.25 miles and 20.62 miles respectively, so matching the I:I.27 ratio of the squared circle diagram precisely.

In addition, several of the methods employed in the construction of the squared circle evolve directly from other prominent features of London's geometric patterns.

A squared circle can be created from the base of a pentagon or from two points of a pentagram, for instance, (Fig 31) although it would be slightly imprecise mathematically.

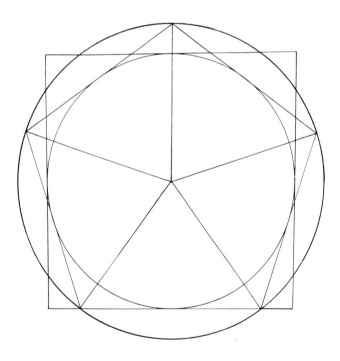

31: The circle squared, although not quite precisely, from a pentagon.

Naturally, the four pentagrams of a twenty pointed star like London's could instantly create a squared circle of this kind, by simply connecting eight of the twenty points (Fig 32). The difference between this construction and London's geometry is that this twenty pointed star is contained within the outer circle rather than the inner.

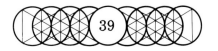

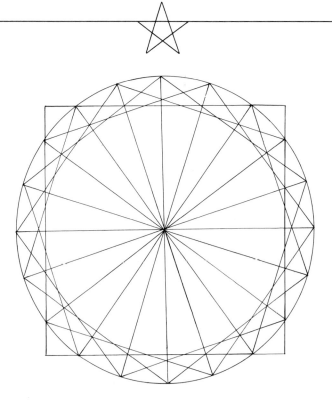

32: The squared circle constructed from a twenty pointed star.

An identical construction to London's and one that is more mathematically precise develops from a double pentagram or decagram on the inner circle. Centre a compass on any of the points, set its radius at the fourth point around the circle's circumference in either direction, then draw an arc across the circle. Repeat the process commencing at the point diametrically opposite the first (Fig 33). Where the two arcs intersect gives you the diameter of the outer circle (Fig 34). It is then a simple matter to construct its equal square on the initial circle (Fig 35).

When this square is superimposed over London's other patterns, it actually turns up some very significant sites. The N.E. corner is Grimston's Oak, a venerable landmark at the junction of four paths in Epping Forest. The N.W. corner is a hilltop near Harrow Weald Common Wood and is marked by an Ordnance Survey Triangulation point. The S.W. corner turns out to be a spot called Seething Wells near Esher, obviously the source of a local effervescent water or at the very least a copious supply of the non-fizzy stuff at some time in the past. Whatever exists there today is now the property of the Thames Water Board. The S.E. corner is in the grounds of Chislehurst Golf Club, Camden Park, and may be marked by another ancient oak, similar to Grimston's but un-named. In days gone by, hilltops, wells and impressive oaks have all served to mark sacred sites or shrines, so these four places may embody a spiritual presence that has so far gone unnoticed by today's more materialistic society.

Since London's landscape geometry is clearly identical to that of the squared circle, its symbolism may be interpreted in the same way.

London's square therefore corresponds to the square of the Earth, the inner circle to the circle of the Earth spirit and the outer circle to the circle of the heavens, the universe, the unmanifest or eternal spiritual realms.

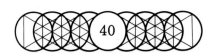

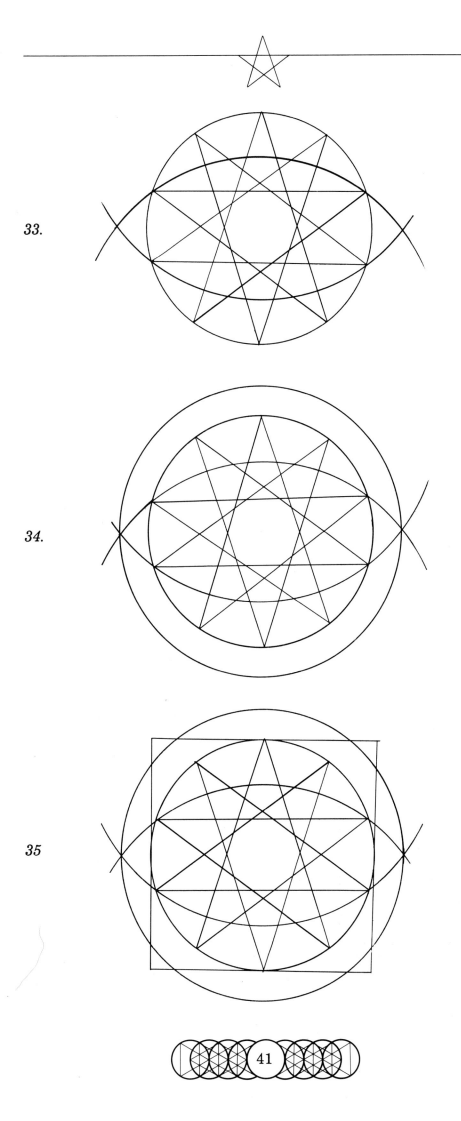

33.

34.

35

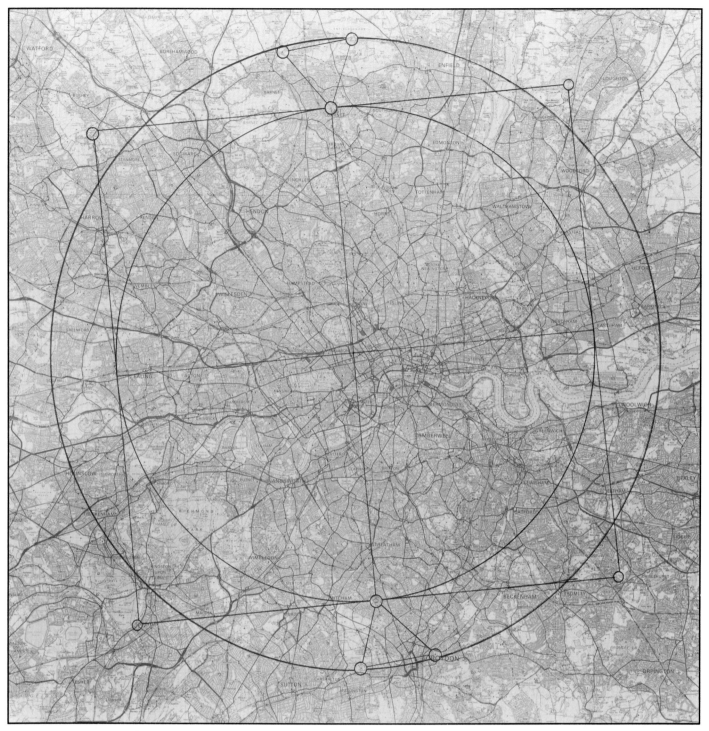

36: London's circle of the heavens surrounding the square of the Earth and the circle of the Earth Spirit

The squared circle's associations with cosmic relationships is not restricted to mere symbolism, however. Sacred geometry is founded upon the detailed analysis and identification of the geometric forms that underlie all of creation. The way in which its principal patterns develop and fit together literally reflect the order and structure of the universe.

Nowhere is this more apparent than in the construction of the squared circle. The proportions of its two concentric circles illustrate perfectly a very specific relationship between the Earth and the heavens above it. They correspond directly with the relative dimensions of the Earth and the Moon (Fig 37).

When the inner circle's radius is taken as 3,960 miles, the mean radius of the Earth, the distance to the outer circle is equivalant to 1080 miles, the mean radius of the Moon.

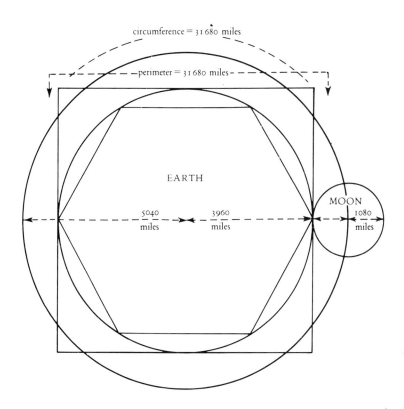

37: The proportions of the squared circle reflect the relative diameters of the Earth and Moon. (reproduced by kind permission of John Michell).

Solar dimensions are present in the diagram, too, although less overtly. The perimeter of a square around the lunar orb would measure 8,640 miles. The mean diameter of the sun is 864,000 miles.

In fact, the more detailed patterns of London's sacred geometry surpass even the squared circle as a graphic illustration of cosmic order and are particularly relevant to Mother Earth's annual life cycle. Its eight pointed star may be taken as the eight turning points of the year which are identified naturally by the two solar solstices, the two equinoxes and the traditional Celtic and druidic festivals which mark the begining and end of each of the four seasons (Fig 38).

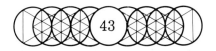

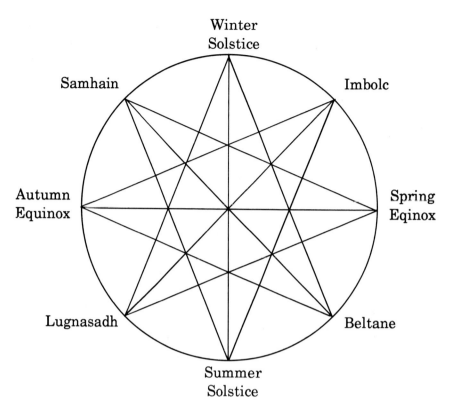

38: The eight turning points of the year. The Solstices, Equinoxes and other festivals which mark the beginning and end of the seasons, the turning points of the year, derived directly from the rotation of the planet as it wheels in orbit around the Sun.

The perimeter of the square within London's landscape geometry is 520 furlongs, a measure relative perhaps to the 52 weeks of the year. The thirty pointed star, since it is on a circle with lunar associations, may correspond to the division of the solar year into twelve lunar months (moonths!) of thirty days, give or take the odd day here and there. When "earthed" to all four points of the compass, London's thirty pointed star multiplies the division of the circle into sixty, reflecting the sixty minutes in an hour and sixty seconds in a minute. Six of its axes would also divide the circle into twelve, to mark the months of the year but also delineating the hours of the day and completing the clockface.

The Sumerians who are generally credited with the creation of our units of time, clearly based them, like the patterns of sacred geometry, on the order of the heavenly bodies . It is surely no coincidence that there are 86,400 seconds in a day and 864,000 miles in the diameter of the sun. Or that there are 43,200 minutes in a month and 432,000 miles in the sun's radius. Or even that there are the same number of hours in a quarter as miles in the diameter of the moon. Like all traditional units of metrology such as the foot, the furlong, the cubit, the rod, etc, seconds, minutes and hours are units of cosmic proportion utilised by our ancestors to ensure that the works of man were in time and in scale with the workings of the universe at large.

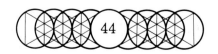

It is therefore an inescapable fact that the basic geometric patterns defined by London's sacred sites embody correspondences that link directly to the structure of the Earth and the universe.

They are not simple geometry, but the divine designs of sacred geometry. The forces they represent have to be understood as the influences that determine creation in any stage of development from a single molecule to the multiplicity of forms within the natural world around us. They are a manifestation of the creative impulse that formed the entire universe.

However, whilst their ultimate expression lies in unimaginable complexity, their geometric origins are ridiculously simple. At the root of the entire process is a single, simple design from which everything else derives; the interpenetrating circles of the vesica piscis (Fig 39).

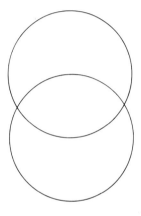

39: The interconnecting circles of the vesica piscis. One of the fundamental building blocks of sacred geometry.

Its construction isn't at all complex, being formed by two circles whose circumferences intersect their respective centres. Nevertheless, it is both the single most important figure and the most fundamental building block of sacred geometry.

The reason for this is the circle's associations with the infinite and the unmanifest. Whereas the hexagram, pentagram, octagon, etc, may be understood as the various forms through which divine force manifests physically, the circle and its multiples like the vesica are taken to illustrate the process at a stage nearer its source. They are suggestive of the unmanifest spiritual impulse behind these forms.

This assertion is not without some foundation in practice. The primary energy patterns underlying nature's physical forms can all be shown to evolve from the simple beginnings of the circle and the vesica. The origin of all form is the point of the centre with its infinite potential for evolution in any direction whatsoever. It is the source, the seed, the nucleus at the centre of its atom, the sun at the centre of its planetary system.

The vesica then represents the primary division of universal unity into its polarised dual aspects, the first step on the road to multiplicity, a graphic illustration of how the one begins to become the all.

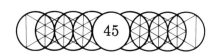

Ideally, the vesica's two circles should be constructed within a third to demonstrate that the progression of unity to duality is an internal division and so can never be an external development. The two circles of the vesica piscis intersect at four points, including their centres. Those four points hold the key to two of the most significant geometric figures behind physical form, the pentagram and the hexagram.

The two points of intersection between the circumferences are perfectly positioned to aid the creation of the hexagram when connected to the ends of the axis through the centres (Figs 40, 41 & 42). The remaining two points, the twin junctions of circumference and centre, are ideally located to serve as accurate guidelines for the construction of two interpenetrating pentagrams (Figs 43, 44 & 45).

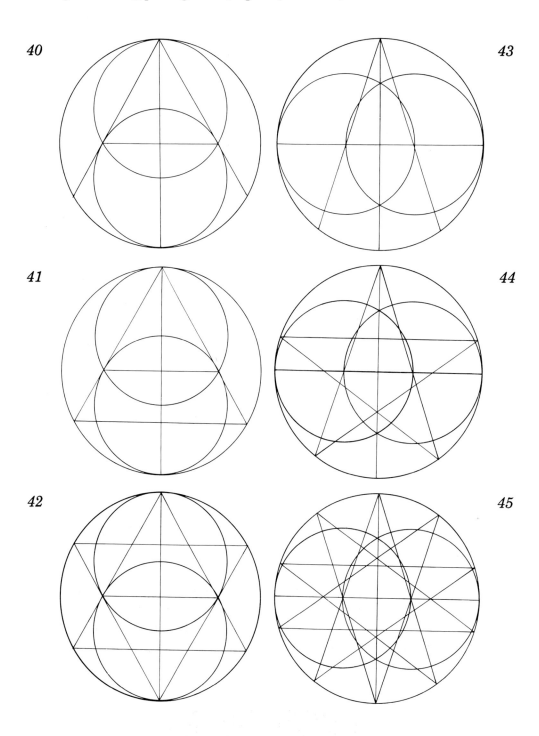

So a simple vesica, a symbol of duality within the cosmos, reveals itself as the key to the two primary geometric forms behind nature's creations. Think of them as the two primary polarities through which divine energy functions throughout the universe. The hexagram and pentagram are male and female, yin and yang, positive and negative, lunar and solar, not to mention any other suitable pairs of opposites.

46: The two primary polarities through which divine energy functions throughout the Universe.

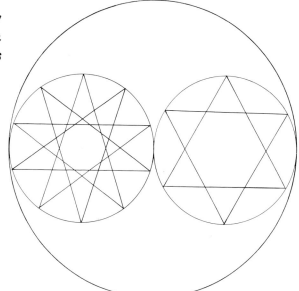

47: One becomes two, then three.

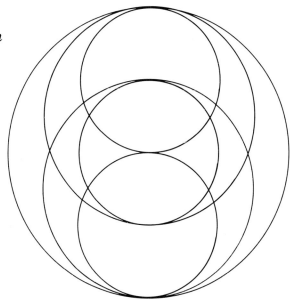

However, to appreciate more fully the role played by these figures in the structure and growth of physical form, it is necessary to continue their geometric progression.

If we put together some more complex combinations of this pattern, it becomes obvious that the vesica generates its own geometric energy polarities by combining and multiplying repeatedly in alternate groups of two and three (Figs 47 & 48).

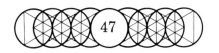

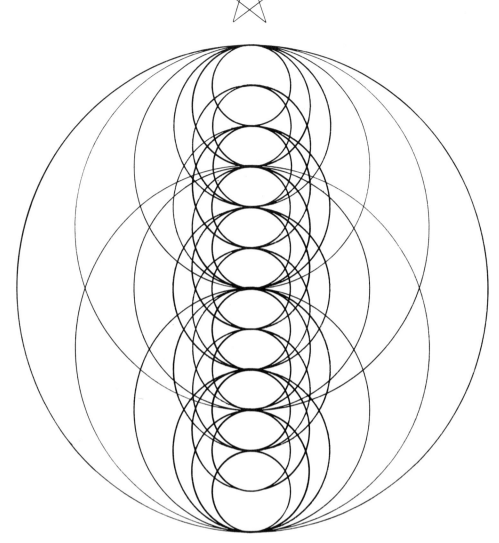

48: The smallest parts are made in the image of the whole.

In these patterns, the essential unity of all life is readily apparent. The smallest parts are made in the image of the whole. They are one and the same, perfectly illustrating the mystics' view that every part of creation, from the minute to the massive, is a reflection of the complete structure.

In terms of sacred geometry, this design is probably the nearest anyone might come to a representation of the unmanifest spiritual impulse from which all of creation springs. So it may be more than a coincidence that it bears a striking resemblance to the spirals of the DNA double helix which modern science informs us is the basis of life here on Earth.

In the past, it has also inspired the design of Hermes' staff of life, around which two serpents are entwined to represent the dual polarities of the universal life force.

The diagram also throws a lot of light on the way the the geometric expression of those forces, the energy patterns of the hexagram and pentagram, exert their influence on growth and form. They work throughout the structure in ways that are entirely in keeping with the expected attributes of their respective polarities.

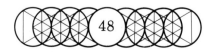

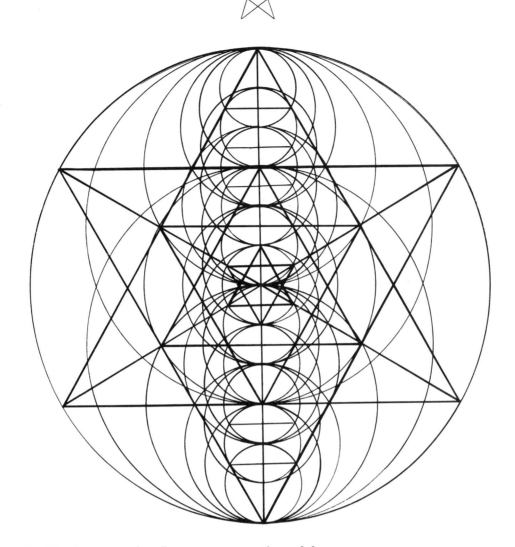

49: The hexagonal influence on growth and form.

The male impulse of the hexagram acts directly through a sequence of positive, logical connections. The female polarity, working through pentagonal symmetry and its balanced form the decagram, functions in a far less obvious fashion. It's a much subtler influence, gently guiding and moulding form and development discreetly and indirectly from within. Its geometric connections are therefore not always as precise as the hexagram's.

In addition to their polarised aspects, both the hexagram and decagram may be considered as images of unity in themselves, their respective interpenetrating pentagrams and triangles symbolising the harmonious balance between opposing principles or forces working through the same geometric circuitry on a variety of different levels. They are primary energy patterns, existing within all things and on all planes of existence.

We shouldn't be at all surprised to find evidence of them at work within the English countryside, nor for that matter the rest of the world. In terms of planetary patterns, the hexagram carries the male polarity which has an affinity to the solar impulse, whilst the pentagram is the

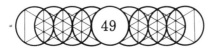

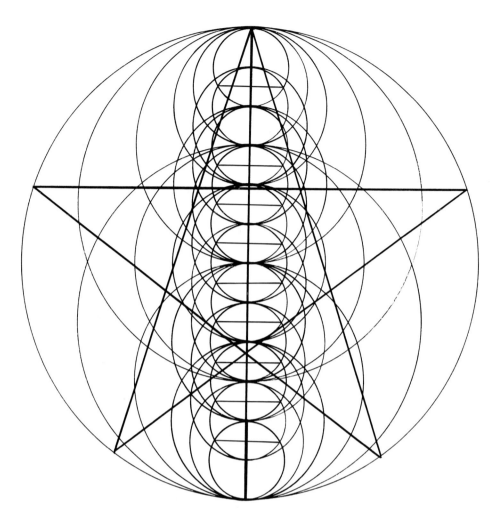

50: The pentagonal influence behind symmetrical growth.

female, Earth energy.

Ancient creation myths the world over personify them as the sky father and Earth mother from whose union all life on this planet sprung.

Operating behind these two, we may also discern a third energy pattern. Its primary form is the equal armed cross, but it extends into a rectilinear grid and relates directly to the symbolism of quadruplicity previously mentioned in this chapter, the manifestation of spiritual force in physical form, the earthing of divine energy in matter.

As the basis of the four points of the compass, it is a direct expression of the Earth's primary physical energies, its biomagnetic field. When represented as the four seasons, it is the background upon which all events on Earth are painted. In fact, in terms of the way this energy pattern functions alongside the hexagram and pentagram on a planetary level, it could be regarded literally as a kind of 'earth', a stabilising influence, a base upon which the other two can interact.

Initially, the notion that various geometric shapes can act as channels for some otherwise elusive energies may seem a little unlikely to say the least, but it can be easily put to the test with the aid of a cardboard scale

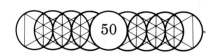

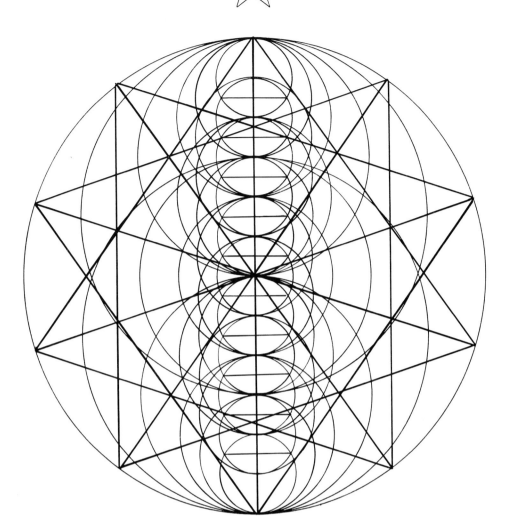

51: The pentagonal influence acting through its more balanced form of the ten pointed star.

model of the Great Pyramid of Cheops.

Provided you align its four sides correctly on a north-south, east-west basis, it'll focus forces that have a variety of unusual, yet well-documented, effects on objects placed under it. It will re-sharpen blunt razor blades and lengthen the useful life of sharp ones. It will slow down the de-composition of fresh foods and preserve some perishables indefinitely. It will even increase the growth rate of seeds and small plants.

No matter what other impressive shapes you fold a bit of old cardboard into, you won't achieve the same results. The effects are entirely dependant on the geometric shape and proportions of the pyramid and its correct alignment to the Earth's geomagnetic energies.

The hypothesis that some kind of enigmatic energy might flow through the Earth as well as through certain geometric designs is also supported by a wealth of independent evidence, the bulk of it coming from dowsers who have repeatedly detected the presence of unusual energy currents, both below and above ground.

Although they have assorted opinions on the subject of what exactly this energy is, they're all absolutely certain about where it is. Most

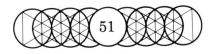

noticeably, they locate it at standing stones and other megalithic monuments, earthworks, barrows, tumuli and old churches, plus an assortment of other ancient or interesting sites. Moreover, they inform us that it can be found flowing between them, making unseen connections across the landscape.

Unseen or not, these connections can be plotted on maps and verified on the ground. The first such alignments to arouse any sort of public interest were, of course, Watkins' troublesome leys, simple straight lines of four or more sites, usually stretching for a few miles across the countryside.

Obviously, ley-lines and London's star-lines are related phenomena, if not actually two different views of the same thing. However, London's spectacular geometry gives a far more complex and complete picture than any number of randomly located linear alignments and in view of this we should be wary of referring to its star-field patterns simply as 'ley-lines' or 'Earth energies'.

Their true nature actually goes far beyond the current conceptions and definitions of either.

Whilst this book will undoubtably add to our knowledge of the subject, I doubt if it will do much to avert the controversy that these studies seem to generate or indeed to alter their status amongst the academic and scientific establishments which, at the moment, seem to regard them as an unacceptably eccentric area of research. The heresy, I'm afraid, is inherent.

Even when we possess a fuller understanding of these matters, they will continue to retain a strong element of the magical, the mysterious and inexplicable. In many ways, their existence is beyond the boundaries of the material world and our normal terms of reference.

In a strictly physical sense, these alignments and patterns do not exist at all except by virtue of the sites that define them and they are like the tip of an ice-berg, just the bits you can see. There's a lot more hidden on levels beyond the reach of our normal modes of perception.

As many previous researchers of the subject have found, ley-lines and their associated enigmas lend themselves to a subjective, intuitive grasp of their origins, functions and purpose a lot more easily than they yield to objective, scientific analysis. This is only the be expected. The nature of the sites involved clearly indicates that they are fundamentally tied up in the spiritual affairs of humanity and may be more readily understood from that perspective.

Nor are they limited to London, Britain, or even the Earth. They have inescapable cosmic connections. They are a manifestation of the formative forces of creation, the life-force, not just of this planet, but of the entire universe.

The ultimate power source.

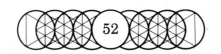

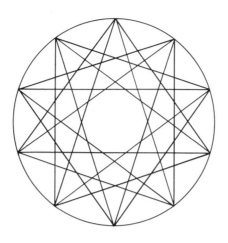

CHAPTER THREE

TEMPLES OF THE STARS

Sacred geometry has some other fascinating practical applications, too. There's a wealth of evidence to suggest that it has been utilised it in the design and construction of sacred sites for thousand of years.

In Keith Critchlow's book *'Time Stands Still'* , he tells us that the earliest written records relating to temple construction are to be found in an ancient Hindu manuscript called the Manasara Shilpa Shastra. It actually gives detailed instructions of the geometric processes necessary to lay out the site of a temple, accurately aligned to the four cardinal points.

The method itself is a variation on chapter two's squared circle constructions. It begins at a single central point, traces a circle around it, then uses the vesica piscis, sacred geometry's basic building block, to divide it into four and create a square, symbolically transforming the circle of heaven into the four corners of the Earth and establishing a small plot of holy ground upon which the temple may stand. All done, apparently, by means of a simple trammel (compass) made from a length of rope with a wooden stake at either end .

52-56: (Reproduced from Keith Critchlow's original illustrations in Time Stand Still.)

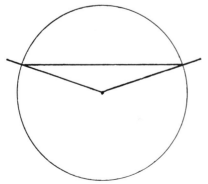

52: First, an upright pillar or stake known as a gnomon was erected at the centre of the chosen site. A length of rope twice as long as the gnomon was then attached to it and used as a trammel to trace a circle round it. At sunrise and sunset the the shadow of the gnomon intersected the circumference of the circle at two points which could be joined up to give an accurate east west axis.

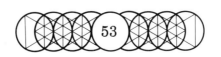

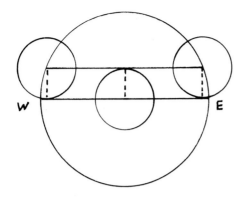

53: *This east-west alignment could then be transferred to the centre of the circle simply by creating a parrallel line through the gnomon.*

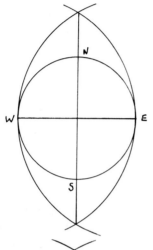

54: *Using the east and west points as centres and with a trammel equal to the diameter of the circle, two arcs were inscribed around the circle. Joining the points where they intersect provided an accurate north-south axis.*

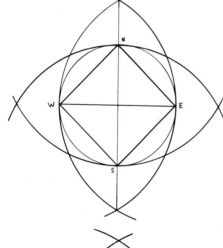

55: *The process repeated from the north and south points to form a second vesica around the circle.*

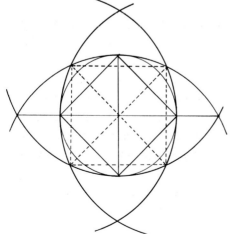

56: *The circle of heaven 'squared' to form the final temple groundplan.*

According to Professor Alexander Thom, Britain's megalithic stone temples also demonstrate the use of sacred geometry in their design and construction. His extensive researches revealed that whilst very few stone rings are true circles, their irregular shape cannot be attributed to any ineptitude on the part of the builders. On the contrary, after examining over 600 megalithic sites, he found that the layout of even the simplest stone rings may be determined by some extremely precise geometry involving the use of Pythagorean 3:4:5 right angled triangles.

Considering that some of these monuments pre-date Pythagorus by more than a millenium, it makes you wonder whether the ancient Brits really were the woad splattered savages that popular history paints them.

Many of Thom's findings are regarded as archaeological heresy. Nevertheless, this hasn't prevented later researchers from continuing to analyse megalithic sites and discover a geometric basis underlying their construction.

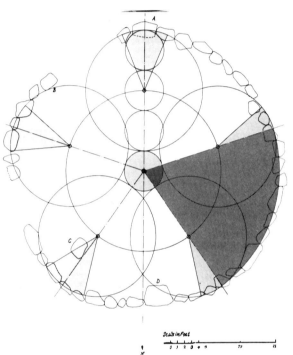

57: Keith Critchlow's geometrical analysis of Moel-Ty-Uchaf stone circle shows that part of its outer circumference is actually based on a series of arcs constructed from an inner pentagonal layout which is not immediately apparent to the casual observer.

By far the most spectacular example I can draw on here is predictably Stonehenge. Not only does it exhibit some very distinct geometric forms (see Fig 58), but some parts of its layout are proportionately identical to London's.

The relationship between the outer sarsen circle and the outer bluestone ring matches London's two concentric circles precisely (Fig 59).

As if that is not astonishing enough, London's thirty-pointed star is reproduced on its corresponding circle at Stonehenge by the position of its thirty sarsen stones (Fig 60).

With 4,000 years separating megalithic monument and modern metropolis, the builders of Stonehenge obviously didn't get their ideas from London, nor vice versa. The common ground between them is founded upon the patterns of sacred geometry; London's occurring naturally, whilst Stonehenge's was presumably man-made, unless you prefer to believe the legends about it being the product of Merlin's art.

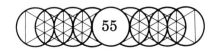

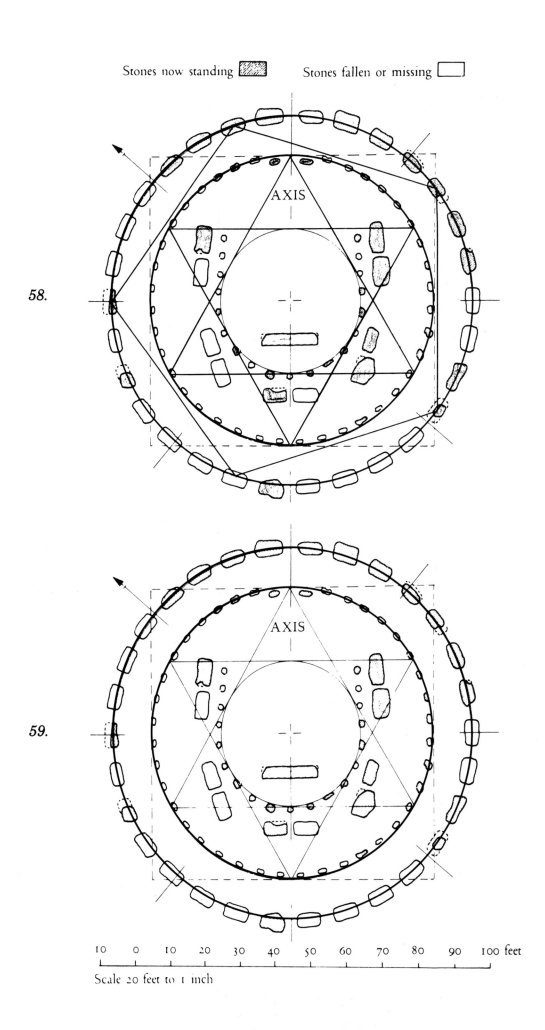

Stones now standing ▨   Stones fallen or missing ▢

AXIS

58.

AXIS

59.

10   0   10   20   30   40   50   60   70   80   90   100 feet

Scale 20 feet to 1 inch

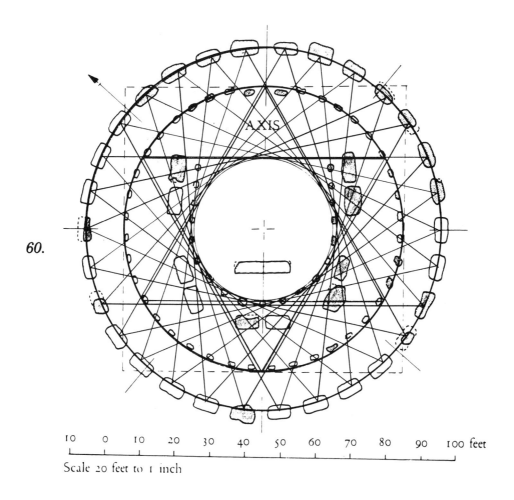

60.

Scale 20 feet to 1 inch

58: Both pentagonal and hexagonal designs were used in the layout of Stonehenge's concentric rings.

59: Two of Stonehenge's original circles are identical in proportion to London's. (Reproduced by kind permission of John Michell and used as a basis for illustrations 58 & 60.)

60: Stonehenge's ring of thirty sarsen stones mirrors London's thirty-pointed star perfectly - and on the appropriate circle.
(note how the symmetry of the thirty-pointed star incorporates the hexagram on the inner circle and encloses the inner sanctum of the bluestone horseshoe.)

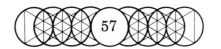

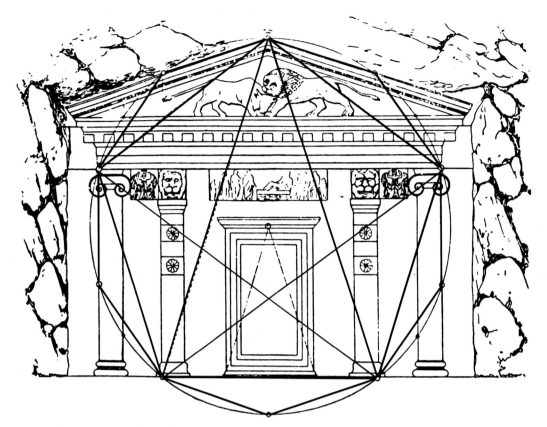

61. Egyptian rock tomb at Mira, clearly based on pentagonal and decagonal principles.

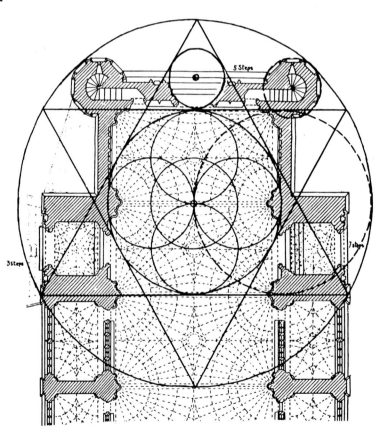

62. Groundplan of the West end of King's College Chapel, Cambridge showing that its geometry relies on the Ad Triangulum system. (Illustration reproduced from 'The Mysteries of King's College Chapel' by kind permission of its author and illustrator, Nigel Pennick.)

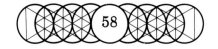

58

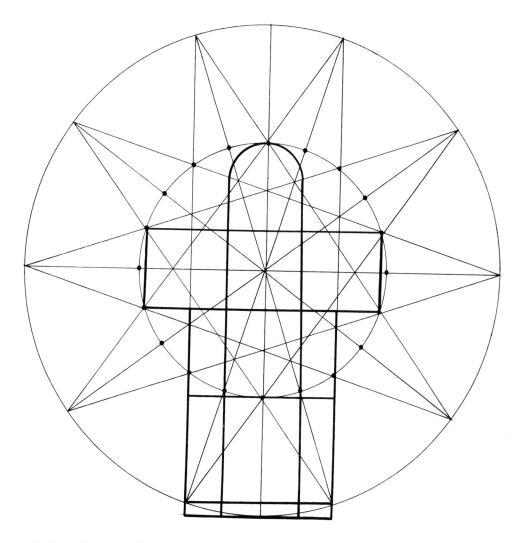

63. *A gothic standard plan based on the decagon.*

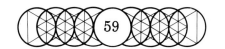

AD TRIANGULUM

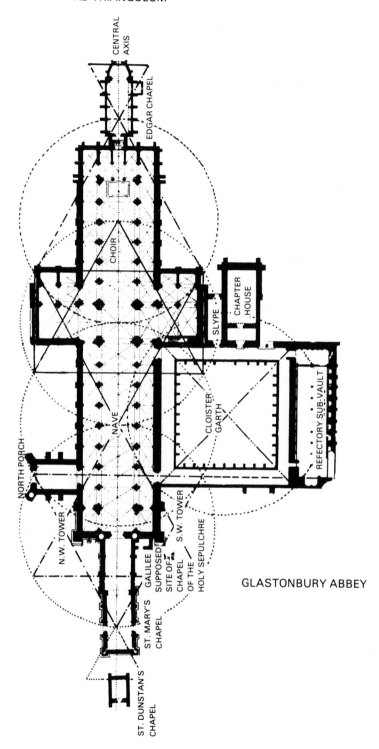

64. Nigel Pennick's Ad Triangulum analysis of
  Glastonbury Abbey.
  (Reproduced by kind permission of Nigel Pennick.)

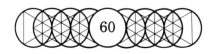

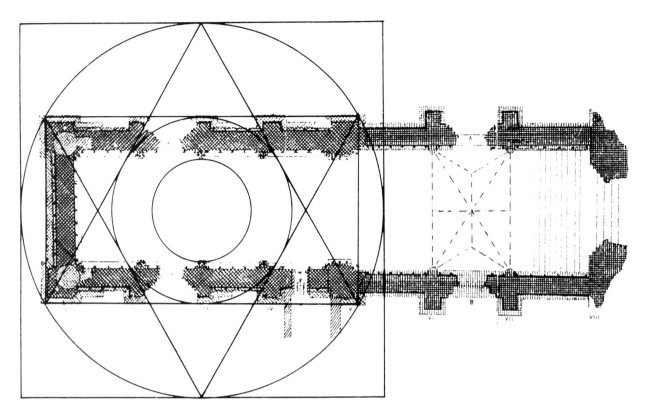

65. The hexagonal basis of The Lady Chapel at Glastonbury Abbey.

Architects of all ages and cultures seem to have employed the general principles of sacred geometry to provide a hidden foundation for the external form of all kinds of religious monuments. Egyptian, Roman and Greek temples with thousands of years, as well as thousands of miles between them, all demonstrate the proportions of Plato's Golden Mean in their design. The great abbeys and cathedrals of Europe, along with Saxon, Norman and Gothic churches can all be shown to exhibit various examples of sacred geometry as an esoteric aspect of their construction.

In fact, according to Keith Critchlow, the masons of the middle ages employed three very distinct systems of sacred geometry as the basis of their constructions; Ad quadratum, a design based on interlocking squares and vesicas; Ad Triangulum, a system of interlocking equilateral triangles, hexagrams and vesicas; and thirdly, a design based on interlocking pentagrams or decagrams, which is less well-documented, possibly because it was regarded as being even more esoteric in nature than the other two.

So all three primary energy patterns of the hexagram, pentagram and octagon were utilised individually or collectively in the design of sacred structures.

Obviously, the knowledge of sacred geometry survived the centuries carefully concealed within successive religious orders, secret societies and masonic guilds, as well as within the structures they created. Its presence in the design of these places of worship, suggests that the architects and

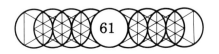

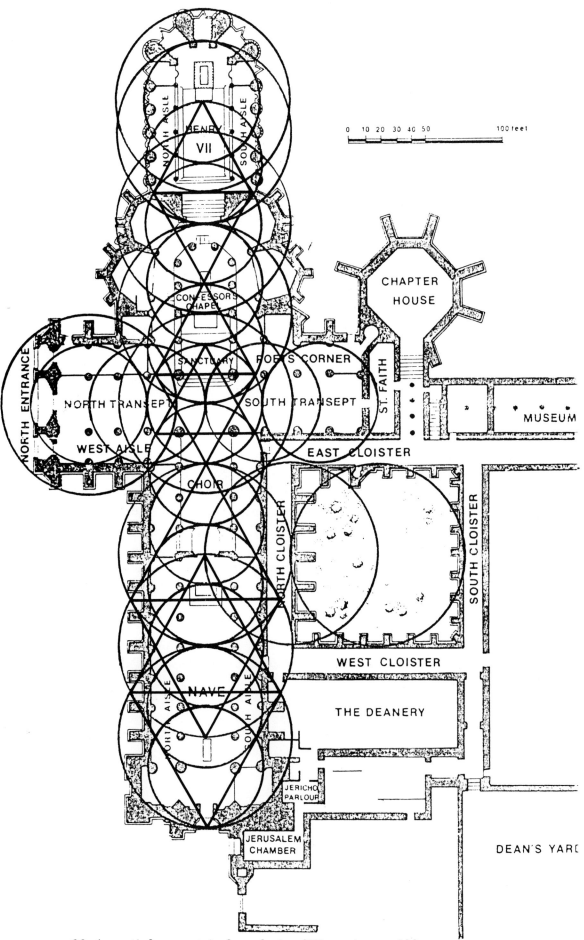

66. A partial geometrical analysis of Westminster Abbey.

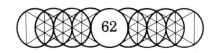

master masons responsible were well aware of the importance of proportional harmony and its connections to the geometric circuitry of divine power.

By erecting their stone, bricks and mortar upon a groundplan of the appropriate patterns, they were building upon firm foundations in the spiritual realms as well as upon terra firma. Thus they ensured that the entire building could resonate in harmony with the primary spiritual powers and act as a channel through which they could flow. Sacred geometry provided the spiritual energy circuits within these creations of man, as it does within the creations of God and nature.

It should be borne firmly in mind though that we are not dealing here with a concept limited to energy, force or power. The circuitry may be live in more ways than one. The Hindu architectural sutras link the spiritual presence of divinities with geometric symmetry: "The divine being is present in the temple by means of proportion."

It is therefore entirely possible that these forces and the sacred geometry through which they function may also have been conceived as the soul of the structure, invisible to the naked eye, yet co-existent within the physical frame of the building.

In a Christian establishment, of course, its soul would be analogous with the Holy Spirit, the presence of God within the body of the church.

Modern architects on the whole no longer consciously incorporate this spiritual dimension into their work. Consequently, when we describe some of their creations as soulless, we are not simply making a subjective statement about the atmosphere of a place. We are being quite literal. They are soulless, the architectural equivalent of zombies. Hardly surprising then that they produce much the same effect in their occupants.

By contrast, the masons who raised the great religious houses and monuments of the past would have regarded their sacred geometry as being of paramount importance, the most essential part of the design. In their eyes, no religious establishment could possibly be expected to fulfil its primary function as a centre of divine power without it.

Equally important, if not more so, was the need to plug into the external circuitry in the world outside. That was done by virtue of the location. There may have been a lot more land available for building in those days, but any old site just wouldn't do. You had to find a place that by its very nature was already sacred. A natural power point in the earth's energy network.

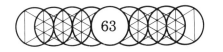

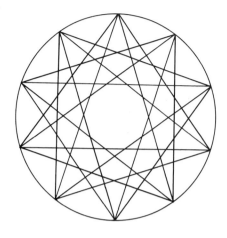

CHAPTER FOUR

THE POWER IN THE LAND

The most ancient sacred sites of this country, its parish churches, abbeys, cathedrals, monasteries, stone circles and other megalithic monuments seem to be built into a spiritual energy system that includes the intrinsic energies of the Earth, but stems ultimately from the primary creative impulses of the universe.

These places should not be considered sacred only to the one particular religion, cult or sect who may have established the site initially or who occupy it for the moment. They are linked directly to the divine essence common to all things and all beings. They are sacred to all humanity, for all time.

Although many such sites were undoubtably built in geometric relationship to one another, this need not necessarily have been done deliberately. It would have been enough to build each one on its own local energy point in the network to ensure that the underlying patterns would eventually emerge to become discernable, in part or as a whole, upon the landscape.

This, at least, seems to be the case with the principal sites defining London's sacred landscape geometry. They cover such a diversity of places, all with apparently unconnected histories, that the probability of them sharing a common origin initially looks distinctly remote.

Their one possible connection is perhaps that they were all pre-Christian sacred sites. Many churches still in regular use today occupy a site that has been a recognised religious centre for centuries, successively used by Romans, Normans, Saxons and whosoever came before them. Historical and archaeological evidence proves beyond a shadow of doubt that in days gone by it was usual to build upon existing sacred sites rather than to create new ones, particularly for those actively engaged in the business of obliterating the original religious practices and beliefs of an area with a view to instituting a completely new set.

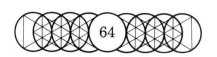

This undoubtedly occurred with every invasion force visiting these islands, including the early missionaries anxious to extend the boundaries of the Holy Roman Empire. Indeed, they were under strict instructions from the Pope to utilise the sites of this country's 'pagan temples' for their own purposes, wherever possible.

Anyone who has read some of the early books on ley-lines, sacred sites and the Earth Mysteries in general, will doubtless know the much-quoted letter Pope Gregory dispatched to Abbott Mellitus in 601 AD, containing some very specific orders for Saint Augustine who was at that time in England doing his utmost to convert our supposedly heathen ancestors. For the benefit of those who do not know it and with apologies to those who do, here it is yet again:

> *"I have come to the conclusion that the temples of the idols in England should not on any account be destroyed, but should be sprinkled with Holy Water and altars set up in them in which relics are to be enclosed, for we ought to take advantage of well-built temples by purifying them from devil worship and dedicating them to the service of the true god."*

Devil worship in this context should not be taken as an indication that the entire British Isles was over-run with practising satanists and black magicians. On the contrary, with the benefit of hindsight unhindered by the religious prejudice of the times, the paganism of the day may be construed simply as the worship of the gods and goddesses of nature, the native British equivalents of the classic Roman gods, Jove, Diana, Mercury, etc.

More to the point perhaps is the fact that a good many parts of Great Britain had already become successfully Christianised centuries earlier, under the auspices of the Celtic Church and in an era when Christians in Rome were still being tossed to the lions.

The history of many civilisations verifies that wherever a new or foreign religion superseded the parochial belief system, the resident deities were invariably relegated to the role of demons or devils in an attempt to discredit them in the eyes of future generations and to encourage the contemporary populace to turn from their old gods to the new.

The various instigators of this blatant mis-representation could not sincerely have believed that these locations were the abode of demons and devils. After all, what Christians today would want to worship in a place which had previously been a centre for satanic rituals ?

The ancient gods may not have survived the passage of centuries, but many of their holy places have, some virtually intact, others within subsequent structures built upon the site. Churches which show evidence of successive occupation highlight the diversity of pre-Christian sites that were considered sacred enough to warrant their continued use as a place of worship.

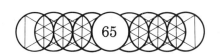

St Winwaloes near Mullion in Cornwall has a row of large stones, clearly part of a pre-historic monument, currently standing in for a section of churchyard wall. The remains of the first cathedral of Salisbury can still be found within the boundaries of a massive earthwork known as Old Sarum, to the north of the present town. Churches at The Bury and Great Wymondley near Stevenage, Lilbourne near Rugby, Ludlow in Shropshire, plus a great many other places around the country are situated on or in the immediate vicinity of barrows or other man-made mounds. St Bride's Church in Fleet Street retains evidence of earlier Roman and Saxon structures and occupies the site of a sixth century holy well dedicated to the Celtic goddess Brig. The tallest standing stone in Britain, originally estimated to be over twenty feet tall, towers over the churchyard at Rudston in North Yorkshire.

On a lesser scale, St. Mary's at Bradley in Staffordshire, St. Mary's at Bayford in Hertfordshire, St. John's at Woodhurst near Huntingdon and St. John's at Cottered, Herts, all have unusual stones, small or not so small, actually in the churchyard, or a short distance from it. Numerous other old churches are built in close proximity to standing stones of assorted sizes, as well as sacred springs, holy wells, tumuli and all kinds of other things that would have identified them as sites of special significance long before the actual arrival of the church.

The first conclusion we may jump to in the light of this information is that a religious establishment with a known history of successive occupation spanning several centuries, whether it retains remnants of its pre-Christian origins or not, may mark a site that dates right back to man's earliest ritual activities when the priesthood enjoyed a full working relationship with the spiritual powers of the universe.

Of the ten sites defining the points of London's four triangles, from which the entire pattern derives, no less than eight fall into this general category. Pollard's Hill is clearly a pre-Christian site, Barking Abbey, Camlet Moat and St. Mary's Bellingham, all date back to the Saxon era, whilst the various St. Mary's at Monken Hadleigh, East Barnet, East Ham and Norbury Green all have a known history extending to Norman times.

Unfortunately, even if all the sites are pre-Christian, there is no reason to suppose that they share any other common origins. Even so, since they are so obviously an intrinsic part of a vast, landscape temple groundplan, we cannot ignore the fact that our forebears were blessed with the ability to locate nearby power points in the spiritual version of nature's national grid.

If nothing else, this indicates that the knowledge and manipulation of spiritual energy and its earthly counterpart may well have been a covert sacred science once practised by the church in its dim and distant past, as well as by the priesthoods that preceded it, the druids and their forebears.

Certainly, if the use of sacred geometry in architecture was a hidden facet of their knowledge, it is not unreasonable to assume that other spiritual sciences concerned with the manipulation of esoteric energies at large in the landscape may also have been on the curriculum for initiates into the upper echelons of their hierarchies. Whether this was in fact the

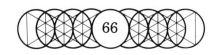

case, or not, it is a plausible explanation of how these sites came to be recognised as sacred in the first place, as well as why they were then so frequently selected as religious and spiritual centres in preference to any new and more convenient sites.

In substantiation of this belief, just such a science does actually exist and has been practised uninterrupted for nigh on three thousand years in China and other parts of the Far East. It's a form of geomancy, or divination of the Earth, called Feng Shui and several authors before me, notably John Michell, Nigel Pennick and Tom Graves have all written extensively on the subject. However, for those readers who have not encountered it before, it's worth running briefly through its basic principles which provide some much-needed supportive evidence for at least a couple of the ideas so far expressed.

First of all, unseen currents of energy flowing across the land are fundamental to Feng Shui and it should come as no surprise to learn that the Chinese word for them, Chi, translates into English as life-force, so fitting in nicely with the notions of ancient geometricians, mystics and modern dowsers alike.

The concept of Chi doesn't seem to be limited to a single energy, though. In the Earth's underground currents, it encompasses two principal polarities represented symbolically as the forces of the tiger and the dragon. The dragon also lends its name to the routes along which these energies are said to flow, Lung Mei, or in English, dragon paths. As a result, a Chinese Feng Shui practitioner is often referred to as the local dragon man (or woman).

Now this is an interesting correspondence since a dragon or serpent is used world-wide to represent the powers of the earth. In European folklore, the dragon slaying legends of St. Michael and St. George echo one of the basic practical applications of geomancy, previously featured in the establishment of the Hindu Temples described in chapter two.

Knocking a gnomon (a kind of stake - but a lance, spear or sword would do just as well) into the ground at a powerful energy site may be seen as ritually spearing the dragon and is a method used to harness sub-surface terrestrial power at a location prior to re-channelling it for some other use like the dedication and construction of a temple. It may also be used to halt, disperse or re-direct a flow of energy that has been having a malific effect on the surrounding area, thus providing another direct analogy with traditional tales in which dragons are often portrayed as a disruptive element wreaking localised havoc upon the land.

The forces of nature, you see, don't always work in the best interests of mankind. They can have negative effects as well as positive ones and the talents of the local dragon man are often employed to divert, disperse or deflect these harmful currents, as well as to stimulate the flow of benificent forces that might improve the fertility of the land and the well-being of its inhabitants.

By and large, a dragon man is credited with the ability to detect the various currents and power points of Chi affecting any particular area, residence or even a single room, by recourse to a complex geomantic

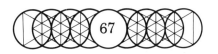

compass or by the application of his geomantic knowledge and experience, or even by dowsing or other intuitive means. To bring about a balance of forces that will have a beneficial influence on the area and its inhabitants, he may suggest a number of remedies, which may vary from re-sculpturing the surrounding landscape to re-directing the energy currents.

Needless to say, Feng Shui can also be used to determine the most auspicious location for a temple, shrine or tomb, or any other construction for that matter.

Generally speaking though, this type of geomancy stems from a realisation that humanity and all its endeavors need to maintain a strict harmony with the workings of nature. It springs from the fundamental philosophy of the Tao, which shares in common with ancient mystical tradition the world over, the belief that all things are essentially one and as a direct consequence, man and his environment are inextricably interdependant.

Anything that only benefits one rather than both will not ultimately be of any benefit to either.

Today's environmentalists and ecologists are currently learning the harsh truth of this statement as they continue to uncover the colossal damage humanity has inflicted upon our world over the relatively brief time-span since the industrial revolution. An adaptation of geomantic principles for the modern world might help re-educate us on the finer aspects of the care and maintenance of a small planet and to help redress the imbalances we have created between the human way of life and the workings of the natural world.

For a start, geomancy at least attempts to ensure that any artificial addition or alteration to the landscape does not disrupt the existing energies of the area, or harm it in any other way. More than can be said for the activities of our less enlightened town planners and architects in the west.

It was perhaps not always so. Several notable authorities on Feng Shui have suggested that a similar form of geomancy was practised in the western world in our more remote past and that it took the form of a kind of Earth acupuncture. Tom Graves, in fact, first made the analogy with acupuncture in his book, *Needles of Stone*. He suggests that the life force, Chi, flows through the body of man and the body of the earth alike, albeit in different forms and that the meridians of acupuncture, the lines along which the force flows, have their counterpart in the energy leys between ancient sacred sites in the western world, as well as the dragon paths of Feng Shui.

Just as human energies can be stimulated by the insertion of needles at a nodal point, Tom Graves suggests megalithic man stimulated and regulated the energies of the Earth, by the insertion of standing stones and other monuments at nodal points, creating artificial energy alignments as well as utilising naturally existent ones.

He suggests that ancient geomancy might be at the root of our folk-lore and its curious customs, as well. Far from being the meaningless remnants of primitive fertility rites, they may well be dimly remembered

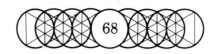

reminders of ancient geomantic ceremonies, often enacted by entire communities, to propogate the generative powers of the land. The peculiar ceremony of "beating the bounds" in which the village menfolk run around the parish whacking boundary stones with a hefty wooden club may actually have sparked (pardon the pun) something akin to a piezo-electric effect, releasing a subtle electrical charge from the quartz within the stones into the surrounding air or into the earth. Another example is our traditional maypole. When erected on an earth energy power point, it would have acted as a gnomon. The dancers who skipped around it may have created a form of human dynamo, their own individual energy fields interacting and generating some kind of localised field effect as they whirled and spiralled through the sacred pattern of the dance.

The bulk of the peasant populace involved need not have encumbered themselves with a detailed understanding of these practices. All such rituals, of course, would have been organised and supervised by the priesthood, which brings us to the principal difference between eastern geomancy and its supposed counterpart in the west.

Feng Shui seems to have been a fairly overt practice, concerned with virtually all aspects of daily life including these days, the arrangement of furniture and probably the correct location of the kitchen sink, whereas the remnants of our geomantic tradition seem predominantly associated with sacred sites, religious ritual or festivals, indicating that geomancy in the west originated as a sacred science, intrinsically bound up in the spiritual beliefs and practices prevalent at the time. By no stretch of the imagination was it common knowledge. It came strictly under the auspices of the contemporary priesthood and, as we have seen earlier in the chapter, was probably a covert practice of certain religious orders, sects, secret societies and other similar organisations in later centuries.

Understandably, there isn't exactly a wealth of conclusive evidence to substantiate these views. The druids and their forebears conveyed their teachings by word of mouth, committing them to memory rather than the written word, while in later orders, all knowledge, both theoretical and practical, associated with these practices, would have been subject to absolute secrecy.

Besides, in certain eras, anything remotely connected with pentagrams and hexagrams was liable to be mis-interpreted by a witchfinder or inquisitor as the work of the devil rather than the application of a spiritual science. This was dangerous knowledge. Those in possession of it could get more than their fingers burnt.

In those days, the church guarded its knowledge jealously. There was even a time when possession of a bible was punishable by burning at the stake. I leave it to you to draw your own conclusions about what heresies that contained. It makes one wonder whether the various inquisitions and witch hunts were perhaps merely the church exercising its assumed monopoly over the right to dabble with divine power.

Geomancy has always been at the root of the ancient wisdom and is probably the basis of religious ritual, magic and witchcraft alike. Since it directly revolves around the utilisation and direction of divine power, it is

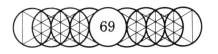

hardly surprising that some of these arts degenerated into devices for the self-seeking, the manipulative and the downright evil.

Something sounding remarkably like geomancy is undoubtably at the root of alchemy, if not the majority of uncorrupt occult arts. John Michell in his book *The Earth Spirit, Its Ways, Shrines and Mysteries,* states that the seventeenth century latin verses of Stolcius relate to *"the grand and oldest form of alchemy, which was concerned to bring about an earthly paradise through the fruitful union of cosmic and terrestrial forces."* A pretty concise definition of geomantic aims in general.

With the advent of Darwinism, however, western man began to regard himself as the pinnacle of evolutionary achievement and our ancestors who practised these spiritual sciences as misguided souls who must clearly be considered progressively less intelligent the further they recede into antiquity. In this respect it is modern man who is misguided. We should not assume that we have nothing to learn from earlier cultures, even those we have been conditioned to regard as primitive. Stupid they were not. What they believed, they believed for good reason.

We live in a technological age, so we understand the workings of the internal combustion engine, the stereo sound system, the micro-wave oven, the personal computer, etc, better than they would. To them it would all have seemed like magic. On the other hand, they lived more naturally, fully aware of their close connections to nature and the Earth. Their knowledge was instinctive and intuitive, not merely intellectual. As a result, it is more than probable that they understood the workings of nature far better than we do.

How ironic that, even with the passing of thousands of years, some of their sacred sciences should still seem like magic to us.

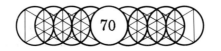

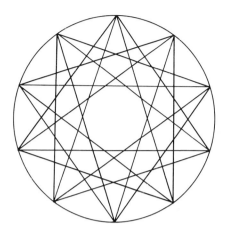

CHAPTER FIVE

THE EARTH SPIRIT AND THE
COLLECTIVE UNCONSCIOUS

Our remotest ancestors may actually have had no need of geomancy to locate their spritual sanctuaries. By all accounts, some of the most ancient sacred sites identified themselves. They were places where the gods were actually seen. Cicero, in his dialogue on "The Nature of The Gods," provides one of his characters with the statement that; "Sacred institutions and the divine worship of the gods has been strengthened from time to time and this is not to be imputed to chance or folly, but to the frequent appearances of the gods themselves."

To put it bluntly, our ancestors believed in their gods because they put in regular personal appearances.

The subsequent construction of a shrine or temple at the spot would presumably be a natural consequence of such occurances and its dedication to a particular deity would stem directly from the specific god or goddess who was inclined to manifest at the site.

That such places did exist is beyond doubt. The Greeks called them "hiera" - a consecrated location where the gods, or at least one of them, were believed to be present in the world. The acropolis at Lindos on the island of Rhodes is a classic example. Its temple, perched atop a massive crag overlooking the cluster of whitewashed village houses, dates back to the 4th century BC and is dedicated to Pallas Athena for the sole reason that it is located directly above a cave where the goddess is said to have frequently appeared. Similarly, Aphrodite is said to have appeared out of the sea at a specific spot near Paphos on Cyprus.

Divine visitations are not as rare as you might think and it's not just the bible and Greek mythology that is full of them. The phenomenon is well-documented throughout recorded history and, surprisingly enough, continues to be rife to this day, with many of the more recent sightings

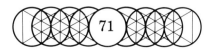

being attributed to the blessed Virgin Mary, rather than pagan gods and goddesses.

On 1061, for example, the Virgin Mary is said to have appeared at Walsingham in Norfolk. On Februrary 11th, 1858, the most renowned visitation of the Virgin occurred at Lourdes, witnessed by Bernadette Sourbirous. More recent incidents have taken place at Fatima, Portugal in 1915; Banneux, Belgium in 1933; Garabandal, Spain in 1961: the church of St. Mary in Zeitoun, Cairo, in 1968 and at Medjugorje, Yugoslavia in 1985, not to mention scores more.

Even today, they are accepted as almost commonplace in certain parts of the world. I recently asked a Greek friend why so many small Greek churches are found in out-of-the way places like the middle of a cultivated field, halfway up the side of a mountain, or somewhere else that indicates ease of access by the local community was not in the priorities of those selecting the locations. I was told that such churches mark the site of a vision, most frequently, a vision of the Virgin Mary, or occasionally, one of the saints.

A good many of our old British churches seem to be in the middle of nowhere, rather than the middle of the local community, so I suspect they may have once been the scene of divine visitations, too. They are, after all, places where one traditionally communes with one's God, are they not ?

Ideas like that are not the product of our ancestors' over-active imaginations. Our remotest forebears were eminently practical folk, concerned principally with providing themselves and their families with food and shelter. If they recognised the natural sanctity of certain places it was as a result of real, personal experience, not flights of fancy.

It is personal experience that has prompted me to write this. Visions and apparitions of goddesses played a very influential part in this discovery. They initially came to my attention in vivid dreams, in meditations or through spontaneous clairvoyant visions at some of the sites involved. One fitted the general description of Robert Graves' White Goddess perfectly - a radiant, almost angelic female in white, traditionally the virginal or inspirational aspect of the Moon Goddess. Another was the Earth Goddess, who would always appear dark-haired, wearing a floral dress and with a kind of halo of bright stars around her head.

In the dreams, they seemed associated with specific sites - the Earth Goddess with St. Mary's East Barnet, the White Goddess with Camelot moat - in fact on several occasions she would manifest as a Guinivere look-alike, wearing a white mediaeval gown, complete with conical hat and veil.

When I visited the sites, I found that I could sometimes sense the presence of their particular goddesses in the atmosphere of the site and in the spirit of the place. In fact, they were an embodiment of the spirit of the place, or so it seemed to me.

The apparitions were not in the least bit frightening. On the contrary, they exuded an air of peace, of gentleness, their gestures and expressions always warm and welcoming. In the dreams and meditations their scale was usually comparable to human proportions. But at the sites themselves, they could sometimes be sensed or seen as enormously powerful figures

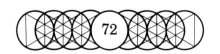

towering fifty or so feet into the air. As none of the more usual visitors and passers-by seemed to notice anything out of the ordinary, I presumed that the images relied on a certain degree of psychic ability in the observer and in my case they were usually a spontaneous occurance, rather than something I could induce at will. It either happened or it didn't.

I deliberately omitted this information from the early chapters as I felt it added a rather sensational aspect which could have detracted from an assessment of the geometry on its own merits. In this chapter, it is no less sensational, but at least it can be presented in a relevant context. It's an important factor, but only up to a point. Psychic and spiritual experiences are totally subjective and however deeply meaningful to the person involved are never quite as convincing to anyone else, unless, of course, they have shared a similar revelatory episode.

The interpretation of these visitations is subjective, too. I was well aware that both goddess images I saw were something which might have been mistaken for a vision of the Virgin Mary by anyone less mystically inclined than myself. So what exactly was I seeing ?

Although some of these old places have their fair shares of ghosts and guardian spirits, these were neither. I felt intuitively that the goddesses were both the spirit of the place and the intrinsic energies of the site, temporarily manifest in appropriate human form.

The gods and goddesses of classical myth have always been explained as universal forces or principles, personified in order that mere mortals might comprehend something of their true nature. Perhaps we should now begin to take that statement a little more literally.

The scientific and academic communities are rapidly re-discovering something that was common knowledge until a few hundred years ago; that the Earth is alive, a vast, self-regulating living organism composed of a multitude of mutually interdependant life forms. In strictly scientific jargon, the concept comes under the general heading of global symbiosis. Our ancestors on the other hand preferred less impersonal terminology. To them, she was Mother Earth.

By all accounts, as the Great Mother, or simply the Mother Goddess, she was mankind's first deity. Figurines taken to represent a rather plump goddess, obviously redolent of motherhood and fertility, are amongst the oldest, ritual artifacts ever unearthed. Some are thought to date back as far as 25,000 BC.

Actually, when you consider that in humans and animals alike, it is the female of the species who gives birth and brings forth life, not the male, it's perfectly understandable that a mother figure should have been initially cast in the role of universal creator.

Even today, the Australian Aborigines, the North American Indians and many other cultures with an unbroken tradition stretching back into the mists of antiquity, regard the Earth as the Great Mother.

In their eyes, the rocks are her bones, the land her flesh, the rivers her blood, the air her breath, the people her children. Her physical presence is the planet itself, everything upon it included.

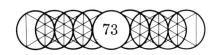

The very essence of any goddess though is her spiritual presence, her soul, and as far as this particular goddess is concerned, her soul was a vital force thought to animate and sustain all life on Earth, permeating all things whether human, animal, vegetable or mineral.

Her soul doubled as the World's soul and life force - the anima mundi, as Robert Fludd called it. Every grain of sand, every pebble, every blade of grass, every man, woman and child and everything else for that matter, owed its very existence to this life-force.

From this perspective, the whole Earth was sacred, not to mention everything and everyone upon it. They were all the physical manifestations of the goddess, embodying her immortal spirit in varying degrees. Their life-force was her life force, the energy of her divine soul.

It may not have escaped your notice that in previous chapters, the life force of the planet was also cited as the energy flowing through the circuitry of London's sacred geometry. The two notions are not incompatible. As I said in chapter three, these energy circuits may be live in every sense of the word. Visions of the Earth Goddess and patterns of sacred geometry upon the landscape, may well be two different expressions of the same force or forces.

That these patterns should be associated with divine souls isn't entirely without precedent, either. In South America, landscape lines etched in the dust of the Andean desert, directly linking sacred sites and shrines, are actually called pathways of the gods by the local indians. More academically perhaps, Plato's cosmology, revealed principally throught Timeus, stresses that the concept of harmonia - the blending of opposites in harmonious proportions - encompassed a soul as well as a geometric shape; a theme, as you may recall from chapter three, fundamental to Hindu temples and European cathedrals alike. Their architects regarded a design based upon the principles of sacred geometry as both the soul of the building and the presence of the Holy Spirit within it, ensuring that the finished structure was truly a house of God.

Hardly surprising then that the same sacred geometry upon the landscape at large should turn out to have associations with the soul of the land, the Earth Goddess, or the Holy Spirit within nature. It is merely a logical extension of the same idea.

This realisation understandably adds an entirely new dimension to our concept of sacred sites and any geometric connections or alignments between them. Indeed, if the forces inherent within these patterns and places are synonymous with the Holy Spirit, as well as assorted gods and goddesses who represent specific attributes and functions of divine force, the phenomena may well be at the root of all humanity's direct, personal spiritual experience.

To understand how this could be possible, you must first appreciate the esoteric perspective on where the individual human being fits into the universal scheme of things and in particular, our individual relationship with the Earth Spirit.

The fundamental error of modern thinking is that we are all separate individuals, totally unconnected to each other. We are only separate

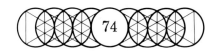

physically. On levels beyond our conscious perception we connect and continually interact with each other and with our environment.

As the World Soul, the Goddess is not simply a single spiritual being. She is a composite entity, made up of a multitude of physically separate life forms, which despite their diversity are nevertheless all linked on the non-physical levels of energy, mind and spirit. According to Robert Fludd, she is the divine mind that guides and controls the world; Mens divina in Mundo.

Within this global energy, soul and mindfield, we humans function subconsciously along much the same lines as a termite mound or a beehive. Just as millions and millions of individual cells go to make up our physical bodies, millions and millions of individual souls make up the collective soul of the planetary being.

The Greek myths explain it somewhat more creatively. According to them, Ouranos, the primeval sky father, procreated with Gaea, the Earth Mother, and imprisoned her children within her. We, the human race, are those children, living upon the physical body of the Earth, enclosed within the protective sphere of her energy body, whose highest levels are her soul-essence. In Edmond Bordeaux Szekeley's translation of the Dead Sea Scrolls, published as *The Gospel of the Essenes*, it is expressed thus:

" Thou art one with the earthly mother .
She is in thee, and thou in her.
Of her wert thou born, in her dost thou live.
And to her shalt thou return again."

Only a combination of ignorance and arrogant self-interest on our part has kept us oblivious of this facet of our nature until now.

Nor is the World Soul, the Earth Goddess, the only collective entity we compose and inhabit. As far as our psycho-spiritual dimensions are concerned, we are rather like Russian dolls, only a lot more complicated. Physically we inhabit a solar system. Spiritually, we inhabit a soular system, if you'll pardon the pun.

First and foremost, we are part of a family unit. Then, together with our neighbours in the district, village or town where we live, our souls are a vital ingredient in the local community spirit. Further up the scale, we are each embodied in the spirit of the nation and in the world soul, the Earth Goddess.

It is no coincidence that the Greek, Roman and Norse pantheons contain gods and goddesses with other planetary associations, as well as the Earth Goddess. Each one may be interpreted as a personification of the spiritual essence, or quality, of the particular planet they represent. The whole lot, us included, go to make up the collective soul of the universal being, within whom we live, breathe and have our being, to quote a well-known book.

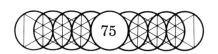

If you find difficulty in grasping the concept of an all-powerful, all encompassing, omni-present God, Universal Soul can be a far more tangible concept, especially as it abbreviates to US. It is us. It is all around us. We are a part of it and it is an inner part of us, hence the odd notion at the root of all gnostic and mystic teaching that we can find God within ourselves.

If all this is beginning to sound as if Carl Jung's collective unconscious might be an objective energy field within the psycho-spiritual dimensions of the Universal and World Souls, you are not mistaken.

For a start, a collective planetary (and universal) mindfield would begin to provide a solution to all kinds of previously inexplicable phenomena, not just this one. Ghosts, telepathy, psychokinesis, psychometry, ESP, distant spiritual healing, to name but a few. In my opinion, psychics, seers, clairvoyants, mediums, prophets and visionaries all tune into various levels of the collective unconscious in order to acquire their assorted insights, predictions, prophecies or messages from the departed.

Although these activities are regarded with scepticism, deep suspicion or even open hostility by many people, they are no more unnatural than a bird drawing on its instinct, the collective unconscious of its species, for the knowledge of how to build a nest, or where to migrate to in winter. Most human excursions into these realms are unfortunately a bit more hit and miss than with our feathered friends. The modus operandi of the average psychic or medium is rather like rummaging in a cosmic lucky dip. You never know what you're going to get and all too frequently, you end up with something completely useless.

Theoretically at least, the collective unconscious should have an unbelievable wealth of information and experience for us to tap into. Every single scrap of human knowledge, every event in every single lifetime is stored within the non-physical memory banks of this vast limitless mindfield, known as the Akashic records in H.P. Blavatsky's Cosmic Doctrine and other mystical traditions.

Through the collective unconscious, we should be able to gain access to any or all of this information, if we so wished. It should also be possible, as mediums, prophets and visionaries have always maintained and demonstrated, to interact and communicate with any of the individual beings who share the collective unconscious with us. That includes our ancestors and other disincarnates whose eternal souls no longer have need of a physical body, as well as archetypal entities like the Earth Goddess and the Universal Soul or being, God.

Access to these inner realms is via two main routes. The more difficult path is through the portals of the individual mind, where one would first have to penetrate the personal psyche's sub-strata in a state of altered consciousness, or work indirectly, as Jungian therapy does, through dreamwork and psycho-analysis. Potentially, this is the most dangerous route as well as the most rewarding, since to consciously enter the realms of your subconscious carries risks to your sanity as well as the promise of progressive enlightenment. Come to think of it, a strictly medical assessment

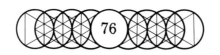

of enlightenment would probably classify it as a clinically insane state anyway.

Alternately, like the pilgrims and seekers or enlightenment of old, you can seek out the portals of the World Soul in the world itself. They are the Earth's sacred sites, places where the spiritual energy field is intensified and whose cyclic flunctuations periodically attain a peak frequently capable of inducing a spontaneous altered state of consciousness in the psychically receptive or spiritually attuned, allowing them a momentary glimpse of non-physical realities and the beings who inhabit those realms.

They are places where the Earth's energy field is intensified enough to sustain a personified materialisation of the spirit of the land, or of the Earth , or of the particular planetary current predominant at the location. In short, places where the gods were actually seen.

What all these apparitions have in common is that they are archetypes that populate the collective unconscious of the world soul. The images vary slightly from person to person, culture to culture, yet they conform to an overall pattern within the minds of everyone.

The Virgin Mary and the Earth Goddess are maternal archetypes, the divine mother. Other goddesses conform to Jung's classification of anima, the subconscious image of the ideal woman. Solar heroes like Apollo or Ulysses are her male equivalent, the animus, whilst Zeus and the Heavenly Father of Christianity are paternal archetypes. (While we're on the subject of solar heroes, the notion of King Arthur as a characterised aspect of the Earth's energies lends an entirely new perspective to the legends of the King who sleeps within the land.) These images are to some extent created by the individual mind in so far as the detail of their final characterisation is concerned. From the standpoint of the universal and world souls, though, they are personifications of the archetypal forces that create the mind itself, not to mention everything else.

The goddess, for instance, does not exist as an individual being in the same way that we do. She is a manifestation of the Earth's life-force, a personified energy form existing as an archetype within the collective mind of the planet and the collective unconscious of the human race.

The mechanics of her manifestation may be conceived as a psychic interaction between the psycho-spiritual energy fields of the individual soul and the World Soul. When a psychically receptive person enters the intensified energy field of the Earth Spirit at a sacred site, their mind subconsciously perceives the energy form and draws on their own terms of reference to identify the particular archetypal force present, producing a partly objective, partly projected psychic vision to which the individual may relate personally. When two or more people are involved, they constitute a group mind which interacts in exactly the same way, with the result that everyone present may report seeing much the same thing. So whilst the various forces that stimulate these visions have remained constant and unchanging since the beginning of time, they will have been perceived at different places, in different eras and by different people as a variety of archetypal forms.

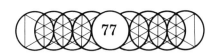

An ancient Egyptian may have witnessed a visitation of Isis, a Greek would have marvelled at the sight of Demeter and a good, God-fearing Catholic might be treated to a vision of the Blessed Virgin Mary.

None of them would have been mistaken in their assessment of the situation, nor taken in by the apparition. The function of that particular energy would have been a benificent, nurturing, maternal impulse and any divine mother archetype would provide a suitable visible expression of its function.

Other energies would of course give rise to different archetypal images and throughout the course of history, they would have evolved in parallel to human consciousness. In primitive cultures, the forces of nature would have first drawn on totem animal forms to reflect their innate qualities. The Australian Aborigines still associate every one of their sacred sites with a totem animal, a wallaby, a snake, a honey ant, etc. Thus a place called Dingo Rock, for instance, will be so named because the genus loci takes the form of a dingo who is the archetype or ancestor of all those tribesmen whose totem is the dingo.

Similarly, the oriental geomancers still have the dragons and tigers that have personified the Earth's energies in that part of the world for the past three thousand odd years. Elsewhere bulls and bears loom large in folk legend and as cult characterisations. Meanwhile, back in dear old Britain, their counterparts linger on in the black dogs, red and white lions, red and green dragons, white and black horses, etc, that feature strongly in local legend, place names, old inn signs and occasionally, carved into the hillside as chalk figures.

At some stage, the energy forms would have taken on human characteristics, initially giving rise to half animal and half human deities like Centaurs, Minotaurs, Satyrs, Herne the Hunter, Pan and the early Egyptian gods. Constantly keeping pace with the development of human consciousness, the gods eventually acquired completely human characteristics and appeared as the familar figures that populate the Greek, Roman, Celtic and Norse mythologies.

Literally, these forces can be all things to all men, not to mention all women. Whether as the primal energies of creation, as the Earth Goddess, as the pagan gods, or as the Holy Spirit of the one God, they are the common denominators at the root of all spiritual experience and all religions.

They have shaped human development and destiny since the beginning of time and they continue to do so to this day, whether we are aware of it or not. The bulk of the planetary populace unfortunately does not have an inkling of these matters. Our present pre-occupation with the material world to the exclusion of all else has blinded us to the reality of the spiritual realms and their inhabitants.

As if to counteract this, the gods' latest act of metamorphosis brings them to our attention in a more tangible form. They are now revealing themselves not simply as an assortment of out-dated deities, but as primal forces that function through a set of geometric energy patterns within the land. Each primary configuration of sacred geometry embodies a divine archetype with whom we can consciously interact if we so wish.

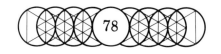

The pentagonal energy pattern, as you may recall from chapter two, carries the polarity of the feminine archetypes. We might safely assume then that pentagrams on the landscape must be the circuitry of the cosmic life-force that presents itself as Mother Earth. In the sacred geometry of London, this is clearly the case. London's twenty pointed star is encompassed by the circle of the Earth Spirit and is the definitive mandala of the Earth Goddess. Its four interpenetrating pentagrams are precisely located to channel the feminine Earth energies into the capital from the four points of the compass. What they create graphically on the landscape is a two-dimensional representation of the Earth's annual cycle of life and growth, the four seasons.

Each cardinal point has its own traditional associations with the four alchemical elements or states of matter as well as the seasonal cycle of the year. East - Spring - Fire; the direction from whence the fire of the sun rises and a season when nature's energies are fired with vigour to promote rapid growth. South - Summer - Air; the sun at its highest, the air at its clearest. West - Autumn - Water; a season of mellowing, of ripening, when fruits fill out and become ready for the harvest. North - Winter - Earth; the end of the cycle, when the fallen leaves, the seeds and the plants sink back into the Earth from whence they came to lie dormant and await their re-appearance in the spring.

The symbolism of the five pointed star is also related to the world of the five senses. Its uppermost point is human consciousness, implying man's dominion over the remaining four points, the four elements and four corners of the Earth.

Earthly power and control on a subconscious level are an inherent aspect of the pentagonal energy field, hence its use in witchcraft. In this context, it's interesting to note that the three largest powers on Earth, China, Russia and the USA, all make use of five pointed stars in their national flags. Of the three, the USA also finds an overt use for pentagonal structure in a building that directly influences the lives of every American citizen and millions who live elsewhere in the world, the Pentagon. With five sides and five floors, its masonic architects, whether by conscious design or not, esoterically enhanced its function as a centre of worldly power and influence through the building's sacred geometry. On the other hand, if the USA's government ever tires of it, it could serve equally well as a temple of the Earth Goddess. Americans already seem to be intuitively aware that the soul of the land is essentially feminine. The statue of liberty is openly acknowledged as an image of the spirit of America.

The presence of a feminine influence also emerges in the sites defining the four triangles at the cardinal points of London's network. Every last one of the churches at these points is dedicated to the same female saint. In every instance, it is Saint Mary, the Christian archetype of the divine mother. Even Barking Abbey, now in ruins, was originally dedicated to St. Mary although the church subsequently built in the grounds is called Saint Margaret's. A further St. Mary crops up on the main north-south axis in the history of Westminster Cathedral. The building itself only dates back to 1895, yet many centuries earlier the site originally

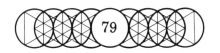

belonged to the Benedictine Monks of Westminster Abbey and, prior to the reformation, was considered ground holy enough to be used for an annual festival and fair dedicated to St. Mary Magdalene and held on her feast day, July 22nd. Inside the Cathedral today, a beautiful 15th century statue of the Virgin has been placed near The Lady Chapel, directly on a spot where London's main energy line passes almost diagonally through the building.

As the majority of these sites date back to the dawn of Christianity in this country, they may well have been built upon pagan shrines of the goddess and later re-dedicated to her Christian counterpart. Then again, it may simply have been the result of the maternal archetype's energy field subconsciously exerting her influence on those involved in the planning, building and consecration of these places throughout the centuries.

Mother Earth's errant children may have lost touch with her, but clearly, she has never lost touch with us. Nor for that matter has God the heavenly Father nor any of the other guiding influences that have nurtured human development and evolution since the beginning of time. They are all still active and moving in mysterious ways through the sacred geometry of the landscape, shaping the destiny of individuals and nations alike.

The Earth, its gods, goddesses, myths and legends are all alive and can make this fact crystal clear to anyone who cares to attune to the various levels of the Earth Spirit at her sacred energy centres.

When curiosity urged me to begin investigating these sites and the subsequent areas of interest they led me to, I was pretty much an agnostic, albeit one who swayed nearer to the don't care camp, than the don't knows. I didn't believe in any gods. Now, it seems there's a whole load of them to believe in, all facets of one ultimate spiritual being. But like Carl Jung, I don't simply believe. As a result of direct personal experience, I know.

William Blake firmly maintained that his work was under divine guidance and after some of the events of the past few years, I think I'm beginning to realise what he meant. From the very beginning, it has been patently obvious, to me at least, that this could not be regarded as a discovery in the normal sense of the word. On the whole, I think it would be more accurately described as a release of knowledge from higher realms of existence, but this is not the place to expand on that.

These forces, whether personified as various divinities or not, influence us constantly through the energies of the Earth, through the collective unconscious of the World-Soul or Earth Spirit and through our individual soul and psyche. They function right across an entire spectrum of manifestation, as disincarnate divine force, as spiritual energy and entity, as incarnate soul and consciousness, as the basis behind physical form. They link God, universe, Earth, man, mind and soul as one. All are inextricably intertwined.

It was inevitable therefore that an investigation into the mysteries of the Earth should sooner or later develop into an investigation into the deeper mysteries of humanity and of life itself.

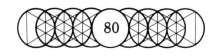

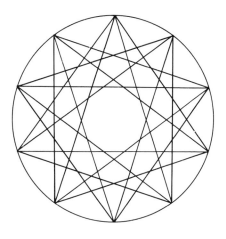

CHAPTER SIX

THE FORCE IS WITH YOU

Many people have speculated that the alignments between ancient sites may form part of a national, or even global energy grid. Unfortunately, the vast majority of alignments discovered to date have failed to support this hypothesis. They have been predominantly simple, straight lines of sites, usually extending no further than a few miles and connecting haphazardly with each other, rather than forming a coherent pattern covering a reasonable area.

Actually, this isn't at all surprising when you consider the nature of the enigma that has confronted researchers in the "Earth Mysteries" field. If you were to link some of some of the sites in London's network at random, you would end up with an apparently unfathomable muddle of seemingly unrelated lines, as well. A meaningful pattern emerges only with the realisation that you are not dealing with simple, straight lines, but with geometric energy star-fields, which to complicate matters further, are overlaid and functional on several levels.

The explanation that these patterns conduct divine energies hardly simplifies the situation, either. Each basic star-field may well conduct a different primary force which, if London's energy patterns are anything to go by, indicates that at least four primary energies and half a dozen others are involved. Numerous dowsers assert that they have detected multiple frequencies flowing along many alignments, so any or all of the forces involved may flow simultaneously through any given single line if it is common to several starfields.

It could all get rather confusing but for the fact that Tom Graves provides us with a key to one facet of the mystery in his book, *Needles of Stone*. In common with a good many other dowsers, he reports that standing stones and other megalithic monuments consistently exhibit no less than seven different energy bands, arranged vertically up the stone and usually with the lower two levels underground. Some of these energy

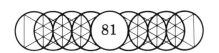

bands are apparently more active than others, yet even those that are dormant can still be detected.

As it happens, seven is a very significant number, particularly where natural divisions of energy frequency are concerned. Light, as I'm sure everyone recalls from their first physics classes, separates readily into a spectrum of seven individual colours; red, orange, yellow, green, blue, purple and violet. An octave in music contains seven notes, too, despite its somewhat misleading name. The eighth note is actually a higher repetition of the first and the commencement of a subsequent series of seven. But by far the most interesting revelation is that the human body also has seven distinct energy levels, arranged in vertical order just like those in a standing stone.

Like so much of our esoteric knowledge, this information originates from the religious and mystical doctrines of India and Tibet where the seven levels are identified by the location of the chakras. Traditionally, chakras are regarded as the psychic and spiritual energy centres of the human etheric body, points where the divine forces that create and sustain all life flow into the human frame.

It would be logical to assume that these are the same primal forces that flow through the Earth and that were utilised at megalithic monuments and other ancient sites by our predecessors. That we share the same basic inner circuitry and spiritual life-support system as the Earth is only to be

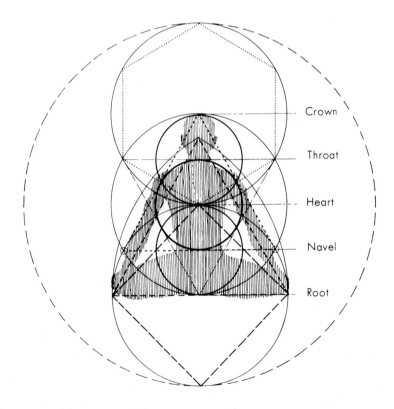

67: The general location of the primary human chakras is governed by the universal principles of sacred geometry.

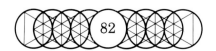

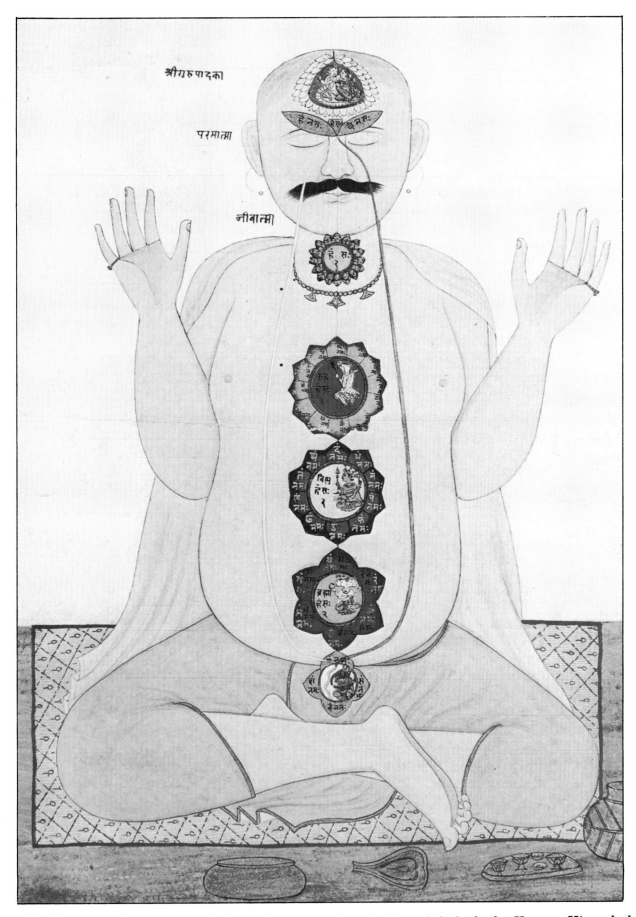

श्रीगुरुपादुका

परमात्मा

जीवात्मा

68: *Diagram of the system of channels and chakras in the subtle body, by Kangra Himachal Pradesh, circa 1820, showing the star patterns of sacred geometry relative to their appropriate chakric levels. (Sven Gahlin Collection, London)*

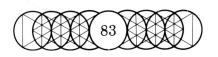

expected. We are not trans-galactic itinerants enjoying a temporary visit to the Earth. We are permanent residents. Part of the planet. We belong to the Earth, not vice versa as our current modes of thought and behaviour frequently imply.

People and planet are linked as one, by the life-force of Mother Earth, the World-Soul, which in turn is an expression, in this part of the solar system at least, of the divine geometric energies from which all things were created.

To emphasise our links with both the spirit of the Earth and other more cosmic forces, the relative locations of the chakras throughout the body generally conform to the harmonious proportions of sacred geometry that dictate form and development on a universal scale.

More important, from the way the chakras are depicted in Indian and Tibetan religious art, it's clear that they have even more direct associations with the familar geometric patterns of divine energy (Fig 68).

In many illustrations, the chakras are shown with sacred geometry's star patterns super-imposed over them, possibly indicating a direct connection to the star-field forces and their different operational levels. Of course, unless you're at all psychic, you won't see anything like these patterns up the front of your own torso. They are actually vortices in the structure of your energy body, with no direct physical counterparts. Although, having said that, they do correspond roughly to the location of the major endocrine glands which play an important role in human growth and development as well as regulating a variety of bodily functions. So in energy terms at least, they may have a direct influence on our physical bodies.

The invisibility of the chakras to the average person doesn't seem to have prevented mystics, psychics and clairvoyants by the score from consistently seeing, describing and illustrating them over the centuries. In the vast majority of cases, chakras appear as spinning, wheel-like vortices (chakra literally means wheel in Sanskrit), or more frequently, as stylised lotus flowers. Either way, the number of spokes in the wheel or petals on the lotus invariably identifies a specific chakra. The base chakra, for instance, has four petals. The second chakra has six. The third has ten and so on.

It doesn't take a quantum leap of imagination to identify each chakra with the particular geometric energy pattern underlying its design and functioning through it, especially when the actual energy stars feature prominently in the picture. The four-petalled lotus of the base chakra is obviously a square, a suitably stable base upon which the other six levels might be built. The six-petalled lotus of the second chakra relates to a hexagonal star-field. The ten-petalled lotus of the third chakra, the solar plexus centre, a pentagonal star-field. The fourth chakra, the heart centre, has a lotus with twelve petals, based upon the energy pattern of a double hexagram or twelve-pointed star. The fifth chakra, the throat centre, has a lotus with sixteen petals, obviously a multiple development of the eight pointed star-field. The sixth chakra, popularly known as the third eye, is sometimes represented by just two petals, and in other instances, by 72.

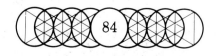

The two demonstrates that the dual primary polarities of man's inner energies are unified through or at this centre. In addition, the 72 may relate to a higher fusion of the energies of the eighteen pointed star (4 x 18 = 72), or the six and the twelve, (6 x 12 = 72), or even the eight and the component nines that form the eighteen (8 x 9 = 72). The seventh chakra, the crown, is reputedly the highest frequency accessible to humanity and is sometimes associated with a lotus of 999 petals, although some traditions put the figure at 960 with a separate central core of another twelve petals, making a grand total of 972. Obviously eight-pointed stars, tens and twelves may feature strongly in the 960 figure (12 x 8 x 10 = 960), whilst nines clearly dominate the 999 figure and also have a role to play in 972, (18 x 6 x 9 or 9 x 9 x 12). Take your pick.

The connection between the chakric forces and the Earth's divine energies is further underlined by their mutual capacity to manifest in the form of totem animals or characterised deities. Each chakra has its own particular totem animal and is governed by its own god or goddess, known in Hindu as a Shakti. Nor are the Shaktis simply representative of the individual chakric energy. Like the Earth Goddess, they are the power personified. Shakti actually means force or power and in *Tantric Yoga* , J. Marquis Riviere tells us that: "The gods, the Shaktis, are not only symbolic; the Tantrics assert that they can see them during their meditation exercises and that they then become " lived through" experiences which are related in their texts."

Regrettably, he doesn't fully explain what "lived through" means, although one might assume that like visions of the Earth Goddess and other personifications of divine power, Shaktis have no permanent existence at our level of being and are only able to manifest in it temporarily - to live through us, or more precisely, through an interaction with our consciousness.

Within each chakra, each primary force functions across a broad spectrum of frequencies, of which only a section will interact with an individual in response to the state of his or her personal energies, as well as factors like age, physical, emotional, intellectual and spiritual development.

As with the appearances of gods, goddesses and the Virgin Mary, the forces themselves remain constant, yet everyone's involvement with them can vary enormously from person to person. Nevertheless, a broad insight into the seven energy levels can be gleaned by a look at some of the known associations and influences of each chakra.

In terms of human energy circuits, for example, the base chakra traditionally connects us directly to the Earth. Its totem animal is the elephant, symbolising the heaviness, strength, solidity and stability of the material world, as well as Earth as the densest of the four alchemical elements. Through its four-fold symmetry, it plugs the human being directly into the Earth's magnetic energy field in the same way that a sacred structure has to have its foundations aligned to the four cardinal points in order to function as a spiritual power base.

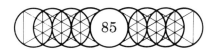

In view of this, it's possible that this chakra may relate in some way to the energy of the Hartman Grid, a rectilinear grid pattern that covers the entire globe and is an expression of the planet's geomagnetic field. The width of the Hartman Grid energy lines is approximately 20 cms, or around eight inches, and this, suprisingly, turns out to be a measure of planetary proportions. In a mile, eight inches would fit exactly 7920 times. 7920 just happens to be the number of miles in the mean diameter of the Earth, so the diameter of the Earth divided by the width of the Hartman Grid lines is 7920 x 7920. What we have here is the square root of the Earth, in more ways than one.

The second chakra is located just below the navel and its hexagram associates it with solar energies, albeit at a low level of manifestation. The solar impulse working through this chakra functions on the level of the animal instinct within man and it is through this centre that humanity connects with the animal kingdoms of the Earth. The behaviour it promotes in humanity is not, understandably, of a particularly high order. It is related to the sexual drives, physical strength, health and vitality, but in both sexes also empowers the primal male urge to compete and dominate which is the basis of much aggression and conflict in individuals and in society as a whole.

Hardly surprising under the circumstances is the fact that it turns out to be the principal energy centre spoken of in the eastern martial arts systems where it is known as the Hara and is considered to be the location where vitality and the life force, Chi (or in Japanese, Ki), is stored. When practitioners of the fighting arts break bricks without breaking their bones, they are not using pure physical strength, they are using their Chi or Ki, drawn from this centre. The energy at this level can be quite primal and may be identifed in terms of mythic greek archetypes with the god Pan or his British equivalent, Herne the Hunter, a personification of the Earth's male, solar currents as half man, half animal and whose appearance and negative aspects served, rightly or wrongly, as a role model for the Christian devil. From Pan, the word panic is derived. In fact, all forms of fear are felt through this particular chakra, which is why fear-related symptoms include sinking feelings in the pit of the stomach and why anxiety interferes with the digestion. Since the devil also thrives on fear and its associated motivations, it is through this centre that his archetype functions in humanity. Those who attribute all manner of phenomena and events to "the work of the devil" would do well to note that this particular archetype comes well down the scale in the overall scheme of things and ultimately owes its characterisation to the dark side of the human mind. In fact, most of the evil in the world is patently the product of mis-applied human energy, power or influence rather than some all-pervading evil genius.

The third chakra, or solar plexus centre, takes us up to the emotional levels of the human collective unconscious. Through it, we interact subconsciously with our environment, our friends, family, neighbours, workmates and with the multitude of other collective groups and entities we comprise. The solar plexus centre is the source of our intuitive feelings

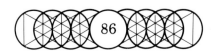

or "gut reactions" to people, places or situations and we often have some difficulty expressing them. Understandably then, it is the first centre that psychics work through, often subconsciously in the case of natural psychics. However, since it conveys vague feelings rather than the entire detailed contents of someone's mind, a great deal of sympathetic translation is necessary to render what is picked up meaningful. In fact, divination of any sort invariably requires a careful interpretation of subconscious symbolism in order to be of any practical use.

The solar plexus centre's associations with the human subconscious means that the energy field at this level often contains a lot of psychological and emotional debris that has been repressed, or swept under the carpet of consciousness. Certain people and places can even develop a severely disrupted field around them on this plane as a direct result of traumatic or emotional experiences. In a house, it may be responsible for anything from, a "bad atmosphere" or vague sense of unease to the recurrent haunting of a particular room. It may even cause physical symptoms like headache, nausea, depression, fatigue, stress or irrational anxiety.

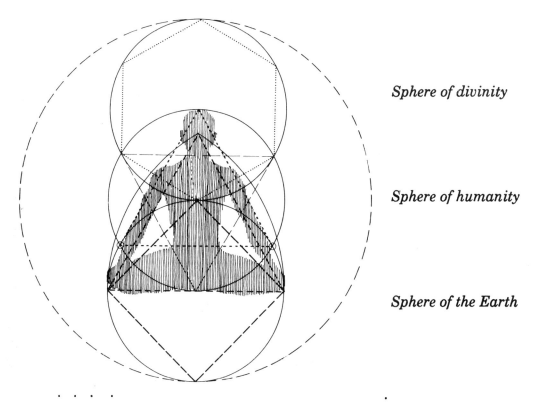

Sphere of divinity

Sphere of humanity

Sphere of the Earth

69: Every human being is at the centre of an energy field which links him or her to the spiritual realms and to the Earth.

As any dragon man worth his salt will tell you, the health and general condition of our own personal energies can reflect the condition and health of the Earth's energies in our immediate environment. This kind of disturbance on a large scale, can even psychically pollute the third energy level of an entire area with potentially disastrous consequences to the community spirit. Fortunately, there is much we can do to rectify such

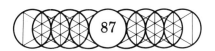

situations, but later chapters will deal with this applied community healing in some depth.

In the normal adult, the three lower chakras we've covered so far are thought to link the energies of man to the Earth. The four remaining chakras are generally considered to be humanity's higher spiritual centres through which we interact with the spiritual planes, the divine hierarchies and with God, the source and sum of all creation.

The point of balance, around which this entire theory revolves, is the heart chakra. It is the single most important point to consider with regard to the balance of your inner energies.

If you are more attuned to the lower human emotions, desires and motivational energies of the solar plexus and base centres, your heart chakra will be seriously underactive and blocking a balanced input of energy to this and all the other higher centres. On the other hand if your basic drives, impulses and emotions are of a higher order, it will be in better working condition. Love, hope, sympathy, understanding, tenderness, etc, traditionally all come from the heart. They are all, in varying degrees, an expression of the ultimate power of the heart, unconditional love.

The heart centre is the first level of real conscious activity and the first level of soul consciousness. The energies that flow through it weave an intricate web between all souls, including the planetary and universal souls, linking them as one. In addition, it is the seat of wisdom. True wisdom is always imbued with a depth of understanding and feeling that has to come from the heart. It can never be based on intellect alone. The knowledge of the heart, the ancient Egyptians called it.

Through the empathic nature of the heart chakra, the spiritually aware individual will first begin to sense the essential unity of all life and the presence of unseen spiritual or angelic beings around us. Above it, through the fifth chakra, the throat centre, operates the force of will, self-expression, the application of knowledge, power and influence.

It governs all intellectual and rational thought processes, ideas, decisions and deliberated actions. In apparent contrast to this, it functions as the centre through which we may first make a fuller, conscious contact with the higher spiritual realms: it governs the first of the higher psychic powers, clairaudience, or the ability to hear the voices of beings who inhabit higher levels of existence than our material world.

The sixth chakra, the third eye, is concerned with the various powers of the imagination and the higher mind. It is literally the eye of the mind, through which we may receive divine inspiration, visions, ideas and the power of clairvoyance, the ability to see, in varying degrees, the reality of the spiritual worlds that exist alongside us and the beings who inhabit them.

Finally, we come to the seventh chakra, the crown, humanity's highest spiritual centre and the point where we link directly to the divine. In Hindu as well as other more esoteric traditions it is through this chakra that we may become one with the universe and its creator, becoming consciously aware of God, or achieving cosmic-consciousness.

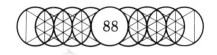

In any rare individual who has attained full spiritual development, the crown chakra becomes enlarged and radiant as a result of the increased energy entering it. It eventually comes to resemble a glowing halo surrounding the individual's head, illuminating his or her entire aura. That's why icons and other examples of religious art often clearly show a halo around the heads of Christ, the saints, and angels identifying them as beings consciously attuned to the highest spiritual state.

In the average person, it is not noticeably active, most people being concerned with the needs of their temporary material existence rather than their eternal soul. But there are notable exceptions. According to Colin Bloy, a healer and dowser of some repute, when a spiritual healer is working on a patient, a column of energy can be detected (dowsed or seen clairvoyantly) descending directly and vertically into his or her crown chakra.

Many healers are consciously aware that they are a channel for divine energy, even if they are not aware of its specific forms. All would state categorically that the power to heal does not come from them, but through them. Ultimately, they invariably maintain, it has its source in God and the Holy Spirit.

A full explanation of the chakric system's yogic, psychic and spiritual attributes and associations would fill several volumes, so I have to shamelessly admit that this brief synopsis may well have overlooked some fairly important points.

Suffice to say that divine forces acting through the chakras control human physical, emotional, psychological, intellectual and spiritual development from the cradle to the grave. They flow through man, the Earth and the cosmos, influencing each in whatever way is appropriate to its needs.

In terms of the structure of mankind's inner energies, we seem to function as a rising scale of frequencies, a kind of human octave that reaches from the Earth to the universe, via the stars of the chakras. This then is the basis behind the concept of the temple in man, every individual's own personal link with the divine. As St. Paul said; "Know ye not that ye are the temple of The Holy Spirit ? "

Humanity, it seems, is not an isolated outbreak of life in a hostile, inanimate universe. Man, Earth and cosmos are inextricably bound up in a vast web of life, an unlimited energy field that permeates, maintains and motivates everything from galaxies, stars and planets to minds, bodies and souls. The universe is alive and intelligent. It knows what it's doing, even if we mere mortals don't.

Sadly, the average person is usually far too bound up in their day to day lives to be aware of their cosmic connections. Their own energies will as a result be attuned to the Earth's lower frequencies, not the higher range of the divine. As a direct consequence, that band of the Earth's energy fields corresponding to and interacting with human spiritual levels, generally functions at a very low level of activity.

The fault in the circuit is not with the energies themselves but with the human connection. We have lost touch with the divine dimensions of

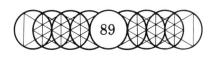

nature and the world around us. We have become insensitive to the spirit of our lands, of our Earth.

Fortunately, in this respect, our sacred sites present a slightly more optimistic picture. Here the higher spiritual forces are operational at a significantly amplified level. Conscious human involvement with them, often ritual use spanning centuries, ensures that they are highly charged. Moreover, their intrinsic energies intensify dramatically around the times of traditional festivals when the energy cycles are at their peak.

At such locations, we can physically enter a spiritual energy field, heightened to such an extent that it enables our own personal energies to spontaneously resonate in harmony with the divine, activating sensory functions beyond the merely physical and often facilitating a perception of higher levels of being. As I said in the previous chapter, they are, after all, places where one communes with one's God.

The 'atmosphere' at a sacred site is a far more tangible thing than most people imagine. In the solitude of a deserted church, I can often hear the energy as a kind of high-pitched singing, hum, or buzz that increases in intensity near the altar.

Those blessed with the faculty of clairvoyance may even see the energy directly, its forms depending upon their individual spiritual development. On rare occasions, I have seen it as wispy beams or clouds of light, often with sparks and flashes of bright colour in it. Visions of personified angelic or divine presences are not particulary uncommon either, in my experience.

The energy can be felt, too, as heat, tingling, or like a mild electric current, usually in the hands, but sometimes in other parts of the anatomy. I mentioned this to a friend of mine, Anne Dalton, one day as we walked past St. Martin's in the Fields, near Trafalgar Square.

"Oh, I can feel it as well," she said. "All up my arm. I often get that. I thought it was sciatica, or a trapped nerve, or something."

We stepped in and out of the energy stream a few times to reassure her that this particular form of sciatica could be switched on and off, depending upon where you are standing. Sadly, the same cure doesn't work for real trapped nerves.

Once you learn to recognise the sensations, you can begin to dowse the energy flows, their intensity, direction and focal points for yourself. I often find that by turning my attention inward at these places, I can sense a distinct interaction between the forces present at a site and my own chakric energies.

By these methods you can begin to make a pretty accurate assessment of the predominant forces at any given site and their level of activity.

On a cautionary note, some of the sensations you pick up, especially through the solar plexus's links to the collective subconscious of the surrounding area can be a bit disturbing if you're not experienced in dealing with them, so if you have any misgivings, or the atmosphere in a particular place doesn't feel quite right, don't open yourself to its lower, human levels.

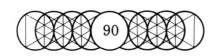

By contrast, a good example of the more enlightening experiences to be had at sacred sites occurred as I walked leisurely up Glastonbury Tor. Quite unexpectedly, I found that I sensed each one of my chakric centres responding as they passed through the seven levels of the Earth's energy bands on the hill. Obviously, this sort of thing doesn't happen every day, being dependant upon cyclic energy flunctuations. I just happened to be in the right place at the right time. But when it does occur, any spiritually attuned soul who has struggled to the top would have had all his or her chakras, including the crown, activated and attuned to the energy levels of the site in preparation for a divine contact at the summit. Presumably that's why the Tor has, since time immemorial, been considered a sacred hill and a gateway to " the otherworlds".

It also explains the popularity of hills and mountains in general as dwelling places of the gods and locations for temples and churches. Mountainous chunks of rock sticking out of the ground have energy bands just like a standing stone, but far more potent in keeping with their size.

Locations where you can enjoy such experiences are actually far more numerous than you might at first suspect. I've sensed precisely the same chakric reactions whilst walking up Primrose Hill in London, a spot which I never suspected of having any great spiritual significance until that moment. Obviously, some of London's Victorian druids were somewhat better informed. They used the summit of Primrose Hill for regular gatherings, in preference to nearby Parliament Hill, a much better-known traditional meeting place.

I've also found that the energy levels in some of the more ancient churches rise progressively along the body of the church, reaching a peak at the altar. Odd to think that you can get closer to God by sitting nearer the front of the church, isn't it ?

The interesting point that now raises itself in conclusion to this chapter is that if the energies of the Earth and of man are essentially the same, or at least structured along the same lines, the planet must also have a chakric system.

Just as we possess a network of energy vortices where we plug into the planetary power system, the Earth, as a larger, single living entity, must have chakras where it plugs into the universal force fields. If so, we might reasonably expect them to bear a passing resemblance to their human counterparts; a system of geometric energy stars arranged in strict accordance with the principles of sacred geometry. In view of this, London's network of interconnecting star-fields certainly fits the bill.

I realise that the concept of London as a planetary chakra may be difficult for many people to grasp. After all, the bulk of the populace haven't discovered their own chakras yet, let alone the Earth's. But if London is a planetary chakra, it could be a far greater centre of power and influence than anyone has previously suspected.

It would make it a city with an vitally important role to play in the destiny of the human race as a whole and the world in general. A city of enormous spiritual significance.

A holy city.

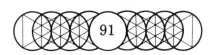

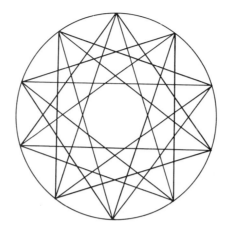

CHAPTER SEVEN

THE NEW JERUSALEM

Anyone who is at all familiar with the many facets of dear, old London will almost certainly find it difficult to think of the place as a holy city. After all, it does have several notorious districts where the impression that you are standing on hallowed ground is likely to be the last thing that strikes you. Nevertheless, its sacred geometry indicates that not only is it a holy city, but that it may well be the new Jerusalem, the celestial city seen by Saint John in the visions that inspired his Book of Revelation.

> *" And I saw a new heaven and a new earth:*
> *for the first heaven and the first earth were passed away;*
> *and there was no more sea.*
> *And I John saw the Holy City, new Jerusalem, coming down*
> *from God out of heaven, prepared as a bride adorned for*
> *her husband."*
> Revelation 21, 1 - 2.

A few verses later, he begins to describe the Holy City.

> *" And he (the angel) carried me away in the spirit to a*
> *great and high mountain, and shewed me that great city,*
> *the holy Jerusalem, descending out of heaven from God.*
>
> *Having the glory of God: and her light was like unto a*
> *stone most precious, even like a jasper stone, as clear*
> *as crystal;*
>
> *And had a wall great and high, and had twelve gates, and*
> *at the gates twelve angels, and names written thereon,*

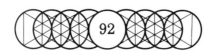

92

which are the names of the twelve tribes of the children
of Israel:
On the east three gates; on the north three gates; on the
south three gates; and on the west three gates, And the
wall of the city had twelve foundations, and in them the
names of the twelve apostles of the lamb."
Revelation 21: 10-14.

Hardly sounds like the London we know, does it? No mention of Big Ben, Tower Bridge, the Houses of Parliament, Eros, the Post Office Tower, Nelson's Column or any of London's other famous landmarks. But then there wouldn't be. They belong to the earthly city. Not its celestial counterpart.

The new Jerusalem is a construction built of the Holy Spirit and has more in common with the soul of the city than its physical appearance. As such, it may also be represented visibly as a plan of sacred geometry. To alert us to this fact, in the various descriptions of the city given in Revelations, particular attention is drawn to its proportions and from these, the sacred geometry may be deduced.

" And he (an angel) that talked with me had a golden
reed to measure the city, and the gates thereof, and
the wall thereof.

And the city lieth foursquare, and the length is as
large as the breadth: and he measured the city with the
reed, twelve thousand furlongs. The length and breadth
and height of it were equal.

And he measured the wall thereof, an hundred and forty
and four cubits, according to the measure of a man, that
is, of the angel."
Revelation 21: 15 - 17.

Probably the world's leading scholar of ancient metrology and sacred geometry is John Michell. In his books *City of Revelation* and *The Dimensions of Paradise*, he examines, analyses and explains the significance of the new Jerusalem in great depth. Amongst other things, he reveals that the proportions and measures of the new Jerusalem have hidden significance for those who possess a knowledge of sacred geometry and allied subjects.

Like most things esoteric, the dimensions superficially appear to be nonsense to the uninitiated. In terms of scale, 12,000 furlongs and 144 cubits could not possibly be measurements of the same city wall. A furlong is 660ft, whilst a cubit of any sort, Egyptian, Sumerian, Roman, or whatever, is less than 2ft. 12,000 furlongs would make the wall a massive 1,500 miles or 7,920,000ft in length, breadth and height. On the other

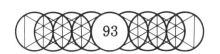

hand, using John Michell's calculations based on the Egyptian royal cubit of 1.728 feet, 144 cubits would give a wall of just 248.832 feet.

The explanation for this major discrepancy, according to John Michell, is that the two measures so obviously reflect opposite ends of a scale that their incompatibity itself is significant. It emphasises, he suggests, that the new Jerusalem "represents both the macrocosm and microcosm, the order of the heavens and the constitution of human nature". This may possibly be hinted at in the curious phrase;

" According to the measure of a man, that is, of the angel."

Where the measure of men and angels share common ground is in the divine proportions of sacred geometry and their underlying mathematical principles.

If we ignore the relative scales of furlongs and cubits for a moment and, reading between the lines, that is precisely what we are being urged to do, we find that these dimensions have immense significance purely in their numerological relationship.

Take 7,920,000 feet, for instance. 7,920 is a number not simply related to how many feet there are in twelve thousand furlongs, but also how many miles there are in the mean diameter of the Earth.

Equally, 248.832ft is not just 144 Egyptian cubits. Move the decimal point two places and it also becomes a measure of planetary significance. 24,883.2 is the Earth's mean diameter in miles.

Whatever its scale, the sacred geometry of the new Jerusalem is clearly based upon the measures of the Earth as well as those of the ideal celestial city. In strictly geometric terms, its foundation is therefore related directly to the sphere of the Earth, or in a two dimensional plane, to a circle. Since it is also described in no uncertain terms as foursquare, with height, width and depth all equal, the figure must also combine a cube, or its two dimensional counterpart, a square.

Now in terms of sacred geometry, there is only one combination of square and circle that encompasses the dimensions of the Earth in its proportions and stands also as a symbol of the divine order of the heavens. It is the figure of the squared circle featured in chapter two.

As a mandala depicting the essential structure of the Kingdom of Heaven upon Earth, the squared circle is the ideal groundplan for the Holy City of God. As you will have no doubt realised by now, it is also the basis of the groundplan defined by London's sacred geometry. Their essential framework is identical.

London's circles are 16.25 and 20.62 miles diameter respectively. The figures may seem unremarkable, but there is nothing at all arbitrary about this proportional relationship. It is as precise and as unusual as the rest of London's geometry. The ratio between the two diameters is 1:1.27. Exactly the same as the ratio between the circles in John Michell's diagrams. The city of London and The City of Revelation are both built upon the same geometric foundations.

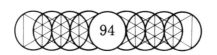

As an exercise in sacred geometry, the process of squaring the circle is singularly relevant to the nature of London's spiritual energy grid, too. Basically, it is the reconciliation of two seemingly incompatible elements, the circle and the square. In terms of the symbolism involved though, that union becomes akin to an alchemical process. The circle is traditionally considered a graphic representation of the eternal, spiritual realms. In contrast, the square is finite and represents the tangible world of physical reality, the four corners of the Earth, four seasons, four cardinal points, etc. The successful blending of these two elements, by creating a square with an area or perimeter equal to that of the circle, was thought to transmute the circle's intangible elements into finite form, thereby establishing an area of Earth created by heaven and equal to it. In the process, constructing a bridge between the realms of divine spirit and earthly existence. The complete figure of the squared circle is therefore a circuit diagram of the geometric energy connections between heaven and Earth.

As an exercise on paper, this may be purely symbolic. As a landscape pattern defined by London's ancient sacred sites, it has to be considered a little more literally. After all, if London's landscape geometry is a planetary chakra, it is not just its basic geometry that's identical to the squared circle. Its function is identical too.

Perhaps, in the realms of sacred geometry at least, symbolism is simply reality observed from a different perspective.

By no means are these the only connections between London and the Holy City of Revelation either. In fact, the more detail you delve into, the more points of comparison there are to be found between the two, adding considerably to the evidence that they may be one and the same.

When it comes to the gates of the city, for example, the sacred geometry of London's spiritual energy grid actually fits the biblical description even better than John Michell's theoretical diagrams.

"And (the city) had twelve gates, and at the gates
twelve angels, and twelve names written thereon which
are the names of the twelve tribes of the children of Israel."
Revelations 21: 12

"On the east three gates: on the north three gates: on the
south three gates and on the west three gates."
Revelations 21:13

It's perfectly clear from these passages that the twelve gates of the city are located very specifically in four groups of three, each group at one of the four cardinal points. The most obvious way to arrange three points anywhere is as a triangle. So the complete picture of the new Jerusalem's gates, constructed from these references, may be interpreted as four triangles, one triangle located at each of the four points of the compass.

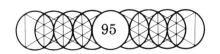

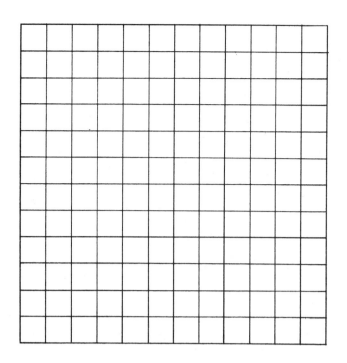

70: *The foundational geometry of The Holy City is a 12 x 12 base grid, upon which all the other patterns may be constructed.*

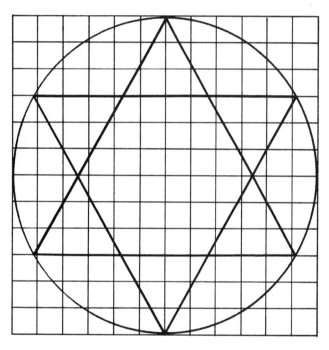

71: *The 12 x 12 grid square provides the necessary constructional lines and points for a perfect hexagram.*

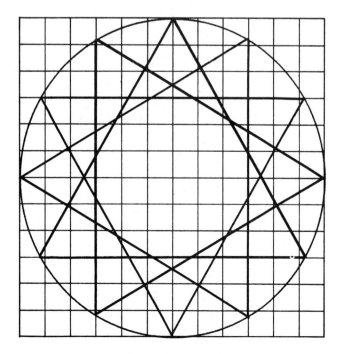

72: *A 12-pointed star may be created in the same way.*

73: The grid lines which define the hexagonal star also provide the diameters of circles from which the five and ten-pointed stars may be constructed.

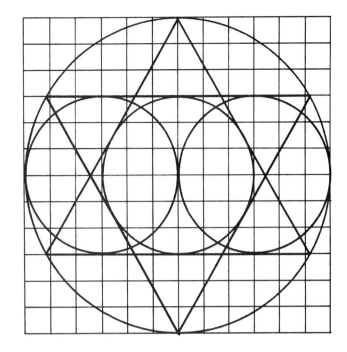

74: Arcs from the centre of the square's outer sides, drawn tangent to the two circles, define the pentagonal divisions of the circle and the diameter of the outer circle (see illustrations 33,34 & 35) thus completing the basic squared circle..

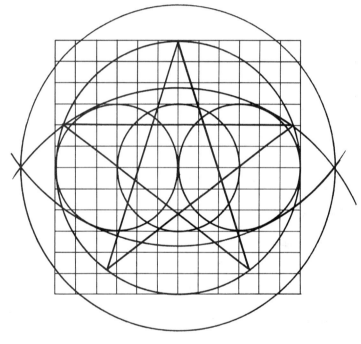

75: In sacred geometry, squares are associated with the Earth, so a 12-square grid may relate to the base grid pattern of the Earth's energies. The essential spiritual foundation underlying it would be this simple construction of circles: the geometry of creation.

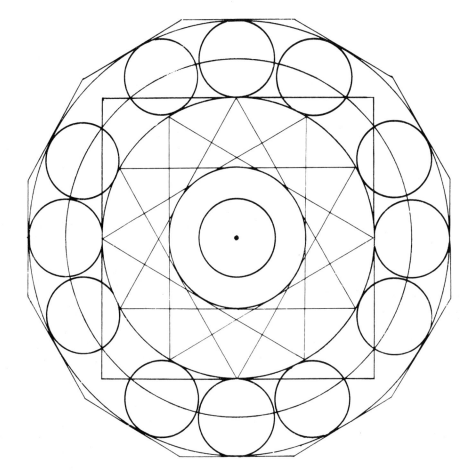

76: John Michell's complete groundplan of the New Jerusalem which he describes as a symbol of divine order on Earth.
(reproduced by kind permission of John Michell.)

What does London's sacred geometry have ? Four triangles, one at each point of the compass. In the north, the Barnet triangle. In the east, the East Ham triangle. In the south, the Croydon triangle. In the west, the Hanwell triangle.

A further description of the gates in Verse 21 also has direct relevance to London.

> *"And the twelve gates were twelve pearls; every several
> gate was of one pearl."*
> Revelation 21:21

Since pearls have many esoteric lunar attributes as well as superficially resembling a full moon, John Michell depicts them as the lunar element in his graphic cosmology. It's an entirely valid assumption given that the relative diameters of the new Jerusalem's concentric circles correspond precisely with the those of the Earth and Moon. However, there is an equally reasonable interpretation of "twelve pearls" that fits London's triangular gates perfectly. The Pearl of Heaven is a phrase often

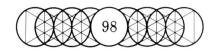

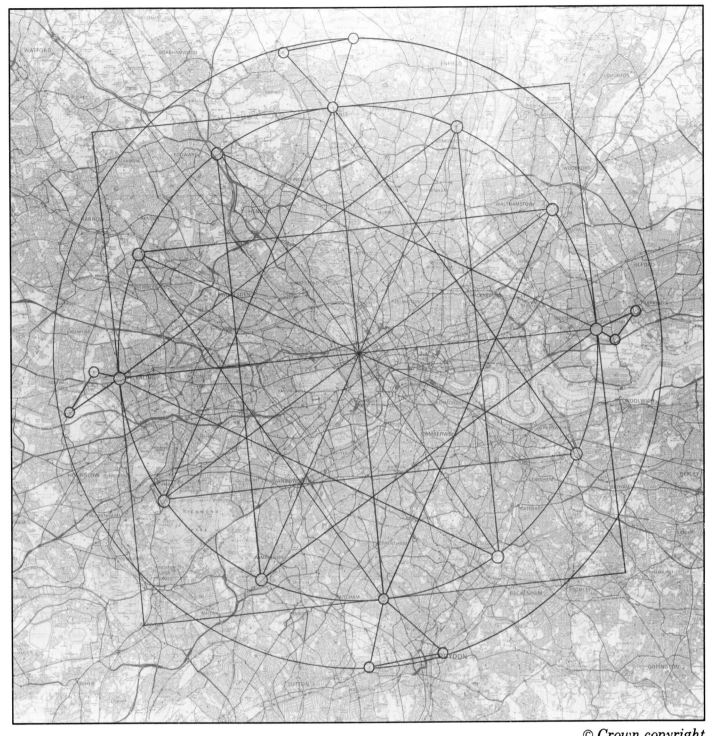

77: One of John Michell's New Jerusalem designs superimposed upon London's landscape geometry.

used in reference to the Virgin Mary. Every single one of the churches that occupy the sites defining London's triangular gates are dedicated to the Virgin Mary. For those with an eye for detail, St. Margaret's which stands next to the remains of Barking Abbey is not the exception which proves the rule. Barking Abbey pre-dates St. Margaret's by six hundred years and its original dedication was to Mary as well.

Harking back to chapter five, the Virgin Mary is a fine feminine archetype to represent the Earth Spirit's divine forces operational through these gates and it's interesting to note that this provides yet another point of comparison since the new Jerusalem is referred to in several sections of Revelation as a female.

" Prepared as a bride adorned for her husband "
Revelation 21:2

Regardless of gender, not only do London's four triangles conform to the description of the new Jerusalem's gates given in Revelation, but they actually function as gates, too. Not the kind of gates that let visitors in and out, you understand. We are dealing here with sacred geometry, the circuitry of divine force. These are energy gates. Each gate is a three pin plug into the cosmic mains. They carry the ultimate power source.

Cast your mind back to chapter one. London's landscape geometry in all its entirety and intricacy is generated by the simple geometry of the four triangles. Their geometry dictates the sacred geometry of the city, determining the precise forms through which divine forces may flow into the capital.

In this respect, by far the most important is the northern gate, the Barnet triangle. It generates and controls the energy patterns of the pentagrams, the decagram, the eight-pointed star and the eighteen pointed star.

The Croydon triangle generates a pentagram and also shares the control of the eighteen-pointed star, whilst the Hanwell and East Ham triangles govern two of the twenty pointed star's pentagrams, as well as the eighteen and the thirty-pointed stars.

Not only do the gates exercise direct control over the specific geometric energy patterns of the city, they also dictate how those energies interact with each other.

The precision and harmony with which they accomplish this is nothing less than miraculous.

For a start, the pentagram and the hexagram, the two primary polarities of sacred geometry and divine energy, are blended with perfect equilibrium through the medium of the thirty-pointed star.

Every single axis of the hexagram and decagram (double pentagram) on the inner circle is shared with the thirty and extend to its points on the outer circle, so ensuring that the circuitry of their energies is firmly connected (See Fig 19).

The very construction of the thirty-pointed star demonstrates its function as a device for the unification of pentagonal and hexagonal forces.

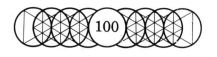

Its thirty points may be shared equally between six five-pointed stars or five six-pointed stars, so it combines them both in perfectly balanced proportions, geometrically transmuting them to a single, more potent force in the process.

That's only the beginning. The eighteen pointed-star combines beautifully with the thirty, too. They share three axes and six points in common, not at random, but regularly spaced. The resultant figure that emerges as the connection between them is the perfect hexagram shown in Fig 21, chapter one. A very appropriate use of the device considering that the hexagram's interpenetrating triangles are universally symbolic of two forces balanced in perfect equilibrium, in this case the thirty and eighteen pointed stars.

In addition, the multiple pentagrams and hexagrams of the twelve and twenty pointed stars are blended with the eight pointed star by virtue of their common alignment to the four points of the compass, as well as a host of minor intersections. (The thirty is similarly aligned but connects directly only with the north-south axis.)

Individually, all these energy patterns have planetary associations. The pentagram is the feminine polarity of the Earth's energies. The hexagram, its solar male counterpart. The eighteen pointed star, the lunar influence within the Earth's energy fields. More generally, they may be equated with the primal forces of creation involved in the progression from unity to multiplicity. As a whole, they form an energy circuit that re-unifies those forces with their common source.

Alternatively, since the energy flow may be reciprocal, a balanced interchange, it would be equally valid to regard this circuitry as a progressive sub-division of the single impulse that is at the source of all creation. Either way, the city's sacred geometry clearly expresses its function as a major chakra in the planet's energy fields, a channel that conducts divine spiritual energy to Earth.

If this is the new Jerusalem, its descent from heaven to Earth is not a literal allusion to its expected re-location. It is a permanent feature of a construction which spans the gulf between the highest spiritual states and the material world, no doubt encompassing the seven chakric energy levels in the process. The highest chakra, if you remember, is a direct connection to God. The base chakra, a connection to the Earth.

There is certainly a preponderance of sevens in the Book of Revelations and several of them, specifically, seven stars, angels and spirits of God, could even be regarded as appropriate analogies for the seven chakras, their divine forces, personifications or geometric energy starfields:

" *Seven golden candlesticks ,*"
" *Seven stars in his right hand.*"
" *The seven spirits which are before his throne.*"
" *The seven stars are the angels of the seven churches,*
and the seven candlesticks that thou sawest are the
seven churches."
" *And there were seven lamps of fire burning before*
the throne which were the seven spirits of God."

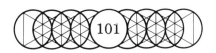

*" in the midst of the elders, stood a lamb as it had been
slain, having seven horns and seven eyes which are
the seven spirits of God sent forth into all the Earth."*

Come to think of it, there are actually seven churches in London's
triangular gates, all dedicated to St. Mary. This kind of reasoning,
however, leads us into some very inconclusive areas and only threatens to
blur the issue.

Regardless of whether London is the Holy City of Revelation or not,
it is a structure built of the Holy Spirit. Nowhere is this more obvious than
at the main gate of the city, the Barnet triangle. As we have previously
seen, in sacred geometry, symbolic form is frequently synonymous with
the nature and function of the energies involved.

The Barnet triangle is a very definite form, a perfect equilateral
triangle. In Christian terms, an equilateral triangle is a symbol of the Holy
Trinity or the Holy Spirit. But just in case we missed the point, the powers
that be have arranged for a second image of the Holy Spirit to be
permanently emblazoned upon the local landscape. It is the outline of a
vast dove, akin to the figures of the Glastonbury zodiac, sculptured in the
features of the area by the combined efforts of nature, mankind and the
forces that work behind the scenes guiding and influencing both.

The dove apears to be flying into the Barnet triangle, the city's
northern gate and the implications of the Holy Spirit entering the soul of
the city, the spirit of the nation, the World-Soul and the collective psyche
of the human race are, of course, entirely in keeping with the appearance
of the new Jerusalem which in Revelation heralds the foundation of the
Kingdom of Heaven upon Earth.

It prompts me to wonder whether the great plague, the fire of 1666,
the blitz and other events in London's history since the time of St. John's
vision may not have been some of the unpleasant events he foresaw in the
destruction of the new Jerusalem's Earthly counterpart. In which case, the
worst may be over.

Personally, I would be surprised if any further divine retribution
befell London. If the city is to become some kind of new Jerusalem, it is
presumably protected by the powers that be as a matter of heavenly
routine. What propels me along this line of thinking is the discovery of two
further landscape figures which will be immediately recognisable to most
Londoners: a lion and a unicorn, the heraldic beasts that traditionally
support the capital's coat of arms.

When viewed on a map, they seem to have switched sides, so to speak,
with the lion on the left and unicorn on the right and their stances are more
suggestive of guardians, flanking the entire Greater London area. However,
their positions on the landscape are perfectly in keeping with their
elemental attributes. The lion, a symbol of solar energy faces the east, the
direction of the rising sun, whilst the unicorn, a symbol of the feminine
mysteries, of divine wisdom, intuition and inspiration, faces west, the
appropriate elemental point for water which reflects the same attributes.

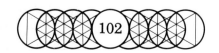

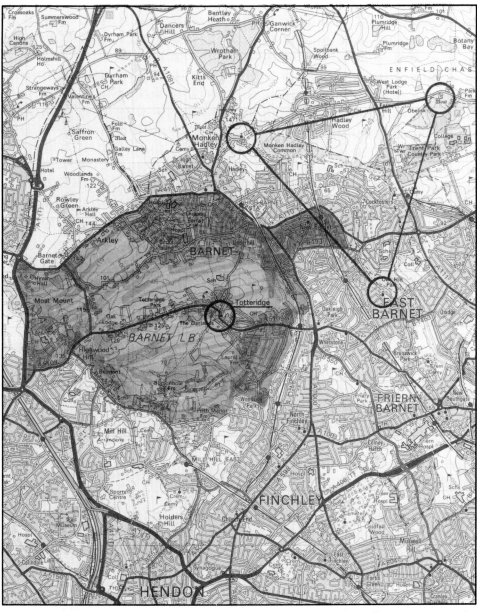

78: The landscape figure of a dove flying into the Barnet triangle: two images of the Holy Spirit at the northern gate of the city.

Again, as if to emphasise that the figures are not there by coincidence, the tip of the unicorn's horn, remarkably, turns out to be a place called Horn Hill and the horn itself is not the only thing pointed at it. An extension of the alignment between Camlet Moat and St. Mary's Church Monken Hadley goes directly to the same spot.

Admittedly, lions and unicorns are not amongst the beasts mentioned in the Book of Revelation, but I think that we already have sufficient evidence to suggest that if London isn't the new Jerusalem, it's certainly qualified to be, on several counts.

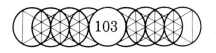

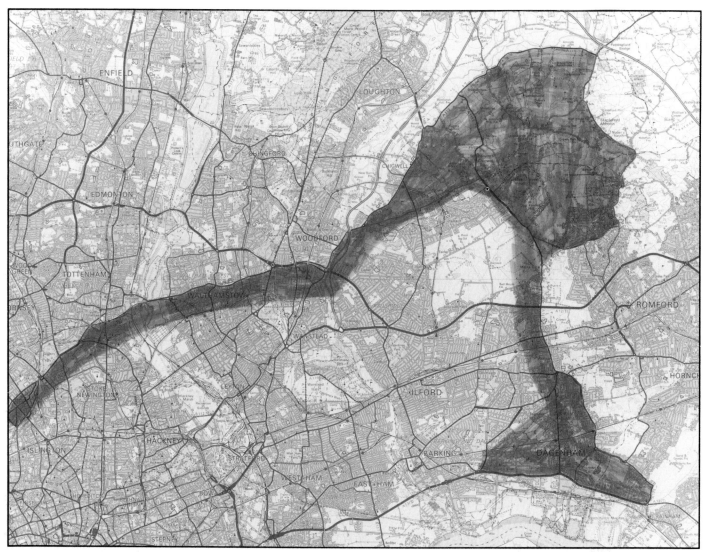

79 and 80: The Lion and the Unicorn, London's two heraldic guardians, not on the coat of arms, but on the landscape.

On the strength of its sacred geometry alone, it is a place of immense significance for the future of the world and the fulfillment of humanity's spiritual destiny. As a planetary chakra, it is a place through which potent, yet subtle forces enter our environment, influencing and guiding the development of life on Earth at every level.

Those forces are at the root of all religious experience and as personified archetypes have been mankind's deities since the beginning of time.

Not only has the new Jerusalem now actually made its appearance, in fulfilment of the biblical prophesy, it has brought with it the dove of peace, laid bare the divine plan of creation and revealed some of the mysterious ways in which the creator moves.

I am by no means the first person to suggest that London may be the new Jerusalem, or city of Revelation. Long before its sacred geometry and

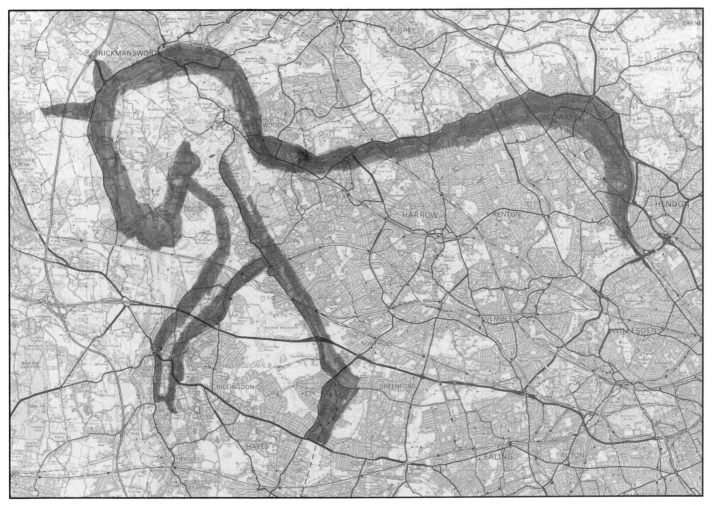

© Crown copyright

landscape figures came to my attention, William Blake put pen to paper thus;

> " *The fields from Islington to Marylebone,*
> *to Primrose Hill and St. John's Wood:*
> *were builded over with pillars of gold*
> *and there Jerusalem's pillars stood.*"

But then Blake, like Saint John, was a visionary and as John Michell says in *The Dimensions of Paradise* :

> " *The new Jerusalem is not a constructed (man-made) world*
> *image, but a pre-existent archetype which reveals itself,*
> *as to St. John at Patmos, where there are minds prepared*
> *to receive it.*"

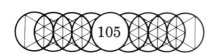

The key phrase here is " where there are minds prepared to receive it." The Holy City is not a physical place you can visit. It is a construction of the Holy Spirit. Judging by the sites that define it, it has actually been here for quite some time. We just didn't notice it before. Our minds were not ready to receive it.

In this sense, the Holy City is a symbol of the spiritual essence underlying physical form, the Kingdom of God within, if you like. It is all around you. You are already in it.

Whether you are aware of the fact or not simply depends on your state of mind, or more precisely, to your spiritual and mental attunement to the divine within yourself.

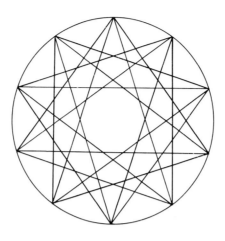

CHAPTER EIGHT

THE BRIDE OF CHRIST AND THE SECOND COMING

It is a curious fact that throughout the book of Revelation, the new Jerusalem is repeatedly described as a female, the bride of the lamb.

"Come hither, I will shew thee the bride, the lamb's
wife. And he carried me away in the spirit to a great
and high mountain and shewed me that great city, the
holy Jerusalem, descending out of heaven from God."
Revelation 21: 9-10.

" And I John saw the holy city, new Jerusalem, coming
down from God out of heaven, prepared as a bride adorned
for her husband."
Revelation 21: 2.

We know, of course, that the lamb of God is a term frequently used in place of Christ. But who is his bride and how can she also be a city?

It's a question that has perplexed many a scholar. But if London is the new Jerusalem, unravelling some of its intricacies has already provided us with a clue to the answer.

What if she is the Earth Spirit, the collective soul of the planet?

As Mother Nature and the Earth Goddess, there are no doubts about her feminity. She is the archetype and role model of all females. Her presence and influence is clearly shown in the city by the dedication of the churches at its gates to the archetype of the Christian divine mother, Mary.

Her star-field and mandala, the twenty-pointed star, is an intrinsic part of the city's geometry. Moreover, it is composed of four pentagrams, which apart from channelling the consciousness of the Earth Spirit into

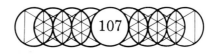

the city, are the geometric symbol for the female polarity of universal force. In his book, *The Magical Mason*, R.A. Gilbert states that the pentalpha, in Kabbalistic symbolism, relates to a female potency which may be either "the mother idea" or " the bride of God, the church, the kingdom."

All are attributes entirely in keeping with the pentagram's newly revealed significance as a power, both in the Earth and in the collective psyche of its inhabitants.

Once the bride of Christ is identified with London's pentagonal star-fields, several other pieces of the puzzle also begin to fall into place. The way the pentagram interacts with the other energy patterns, for instance, throws a lot of light on the meaning of her marriage.

Geometrically speaking, the circuitry of the city marries the female, pentagonal star-field very nicely to the male, solar star-field of the hexagram, a union graphically demonstrated by the thirty-pointed star which combines both their elements in perfectly balanced proportions. (Thirty points can be drawn as either six, five-pointed stars or five, six-pointed stars.)

Perhaps then, the son of God, may be represented as a divine force by the sun of the solar, male hexagram? Chapter 15, verse 16 of Revelation offers some additional evidence in support of this notion:

" I Jesus have sent mine angel to testify unto you these things in the churches. I am the root and the offspring of David, and the bright and morning star."

The Star of David is, of course, the hexagram.

If Christ may somehow function as (or through) a cosmic energy, then it allows us a new and interesting speculative insight into the possible mechanics of the second coming.

What if Christ's intended return is not to be in the guise of an individual human being? What if he is to return as a divine impulse, a force that directly enters the hearts, minds and souls of the entire human race through a union with the collective soul of the Earth ?

Here the fact that the Earth Spirit may also be perceived as Mary the mother of Christ cannot possibly be ignored. As in the traditional Christmas nativity story, we are, in no uncertain terms, talking about the direct impregnation of the World-Soul by the Holy Spirit, a form of conception well-qualified for the description of a virgin birth.

It suggests the possibility that the tale of Christ's conception may, in part, be an allegorical account of a particular divine force and its effect upon the Earth. The son of God is , after all, an apt personification for the first expression of male polarity to separate from the unity of the all-encompassing, universal energy-being of God.

Presumably, this divine force has been active on Earth, seeking expression through the lives of the human race since the beginning of time. It's physical expression is man, by which I mean all human beings.

Under the circumstances, its conscious manifestation through the life of an individual male, living two thousand years ago, or at any other

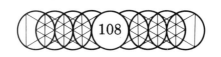

time for that matter, should not be ruled impossible or improbable.

Christ, the divine man, is its highest human expression, a shining example to which we should all aspire and towards which this evolutionary impulse is no doubt impelling us.

From this perspective, the Christ impulse is already here, evolving and growing like an embryo within Mother Earth.

For his re-appearance, Christ would not be born of the body of a single woman, but within the body of the Earth Spirit, an energy body that encompasses the entire planetary populace and penetrates every personal heart, mind and soul. In *Terra Christa*, a book totally committed to the idea of Christ as a living intelligence slowly surfacing through the biosphere of this planet, Ken Carey spells it out quite adamantly:

" Christ on his return will have no need of an individual physical body because he will be in all of them. Each individual, realigned to the divine will, will become the body of Christ. God and Christ will be in action through man on Earth consciously."

To my mind, it's a far more efficient method of accomplishing his ends. Not only does it avoid the possibility of crucifixion, it neatly sidesteps a lengthy incarceration in an institute for the mentally deranged and all the other risks that publicly announcing a personal return to a cynical, materialistic world might entail.

This time, this way, there is not even the remotest chance of anything going amiss.

As a cosmic energy impulse, the hexagonal star-field through which the Christ impulse may function is the male counterpart of the pentagram which carries the universal female polarity as well as certain energies of Mother Earth. It is her natural partner. Her description as the bride of Christ is therefore equally as valid as her role as the divine mother.

Interestingly, whether you regard these developments as a possible virgin birth, or some kind of marriage made in heaven, it parallels a great many pre-Christian creation myths, most of which tell varying accounts of how a union of the sun god and the earth mother brought forth life on this planet, the children of god. What will the resultant offspring be the second time around ? A new kind of human being ? An evolutionary leap to the next stage of human progress and development ?

According to many sources, the Earth is currently commencing a new era that promises to engineer just such a transformation. In fact, quite a few people firmly believe that the new age of Aquarius actually commenced in 1967. If you think back to that time, the sudden appearance of the "flower children" with their overt philosophy of peace and love was an appropriate effect for an energy impulse symbolised by the dove of peace.

For those cynics who may be more inclined to attribute it to an intemperate intake of drugs, I must take the opportunity here to categorically state that, despite what Aldous Huxley and others have written, drugs are not the keys to the doors of perception. Not if you want

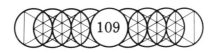

to keep a firm grip on your mental health anyway.

The early hippies' fascination for such places as Stonehenge and Glastonbury, "to feel the vibes" as they used to say, was a clear indication that the new age would bring a renewed interest in the energies and esoteric significance of our ancient sacred sites. These places still continue to exert a fascination that draws visitors and pilgrims by the thousand each year. In the light of this book, it is perfectly understandable.

They are not relics of a forgotten age that have outlived their usefulness. They are still as active today as they when they were first built, possibly more so. As we have seen, they are far more relevant to the future development of the human race than its remote history. Their locations mark many of the major and minor power points in the living Earth's inner energy structure and chakric system. Several of the larger sites are themselves chakric centres, relative to a particular region. Something on the scale of London's sacred geometry, a complex system of sites arranged in precise geometric patterns that cover over 250 square miles, has to be of planetary significance, a portal through which the transformational impulses of evolution flow from the universal soul of God to the planetary and personal souls of the Earth.

The geometric network of energy paths radiating out from this planetary chakra and its individual power points carries the guiding impulse of the divine will through the various star-field levels to the surrounding countryside and eventually, through the global grids, to the whole of the Earth.

We, in turn, subconsciously pick up these influences through our individual chakras, our personal power centres where the spiritual energies of our inner being link into the planetary star-fields.

As I said in chapter six, how the energies affect us varies enormously from person to person, depending on our individual character, physical, emotional, psychological and spiritual make-up, but since we are referring here to elements functioning largely on subconscious levels, most of us are not normally aware of any influence at all. Whether it is the dawn of a new day, or a new age, the bulk of the populace slumbers on, blissfully unaware of the new light and energy streaming over the horizon.

That situation may well change dramatically in the very near future. At the turning point of any age, the energies themselves intensify and undergo a transformation. A new energy, a higher frequency, begins to flow as evolution instigates its next step forward for humans and collective spiritual entities alike.

The image of the dove of peace descending upon the Earth is a symbol of the highest, dominant force currently acting upon the planet. It is the spirit of the new age, Aquarius, pouring the waters of the Holy Spirit upon the earth and the human race, symbolically cleansing and purifying both.

Equally, it is the Christ returning, not in his old form, the man who lived 2,000 years ago, but as the new man (or woman) who may emerge in all of us.

The higher frequency enters the body of the Earth through the perfect symmetry of the new Jerusalem and through other planetary

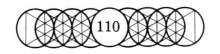

chakras. It will be carried along the geometric circuitry of the global grid to permeate the entire planet. In the words of Sir George Trevelyan, one of the foremost prophets of the new age:

" In our age, an energy that is light, life and love
will flood the Earth, re-animating the realm of matter
raising its vibratory rate to that of the spiritual worlds.
The two will interpenetrate and interact.
So high is this frequency that it will repel all particles,
energies and beings attuned to the lower frequencies of
egoism, greed, selfishness, violence, hatred, rivalry and war.
There will be a total transformation."

On the sub-atomic level, this will effectively raise the vibratory rate of every particle, of every atom, of every molecule, of everything on the entire planet.

In the music of the spheres, the Earth will sing in a higher key.

The lowest levels of the Earth's chakric energies will almost certainly pass beyond our perception, to become the first heaven and first Earth in Saint John's vision that "passed away." At the same time, a new, higher level may become apparent.

In terms of everyday human experience, we may gradually gain a new dimension. What form it might take, I hesitate to speculate upon, but eventually, some aspects of the spiritual realms may be as readily apparent to mankind as the physical world. Whether man might again walk the Earth with angels, as several new-agers claim, remains to be seen.

When will these changes begin ? The short answer is that they have already begun. According to the Hopi Indian prophesy, all the Earth's sacred sites began to activate in 1986. I hadn't given this a lot of thought until I noticed that the main north-south axis of London's network came into direct alignment with the Earth's magnetic north in June 1986. At that time, several key sites which had previously exhibited very little in the way of dowsable energy or psychically perceptible archetypes had suddenly burst into life with powerful energy fields and spiritual presences of a very high order. The simple solution was that they had become energised by their re-alignment with the Earth's magnetic field.

Other re-activations yet to occur depend on the re-alignment of the planet to universal energy fields.

Suffice to say though, that by the time you read this, many more will have had their cosmic time clocks switched on. The agents of change will be loose in the land and active in the collective psyche of mankind, gently influencing us all. The changes will have well and truly begun.

To quote *The Hitch-Hikers' Guide to The Galaxy*:

"This planet is scheduled for re-development."

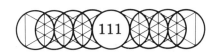

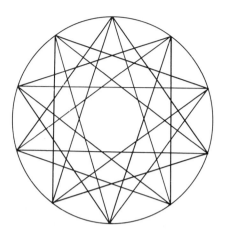

CHAPTER NINE

APOCALYPSE NOW ?

In one way at least, the New Jerusalem is no longer a prophecy to be fulfilled at some uncertain date in the future. It is here, now. It has been here all along, awaiting the correct moment to emerge into the sphere of human consciousness.

Its structure lays bare the divine plan, the interplay of celestial forces that create and compose the entire universe, the inner structure that underlies matter, linking all invisibly as one. In a manner of speaking, it is a map of our spiritual dimensions, the Kingdom of God within. Within the Earth, within you and within everything else.

The energies that comprise this structure are the very essences from which all life springs. Through the planetary power centres, they have been the stimulus behind the development of all life on Earth. Through the human power centres, our chakras, they have been the impetus behind individual growth and development at a personal level, as well as all human evolutionary progress at a collective level.

These forces are the diverse manifestation of the one single impulse at the source of all creation and, as such, they have existed since the beginning of time.

They are our gods past, present and future, encompassing hierarchies both pagan and angelic. They are personified as the characters that populate divine mythologies and local folk-lore alike. They are the archetypes that inhabit the human collective subconscious. Their essence may be pure energy, but they are as alive as you or I. In fact, they are a universal life-support system without which we would simply cease to exist. They are part of us and we are part of them. Inseparably. They give us life and we give them physical expression and conscious awareness in the material dimension. We are the result of their evolution. We are the children of the gods, the offspring of the universal creator, born out of the body of Mother Earth.

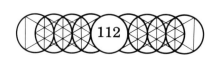

We are created in God's image as beings of pure spirit, divine energy clothed in flesh.

" Is it not written in your law, I said, Ye are gods."
John 10: 34

Working through our planetary and personal power centres, these forces are now impelling us towards a radical transformation, of the race and of the world in which we live.

The process is already underway on a global scale, although the majority of people probably wouldn't think so. The fact that you do not see a different world when you look out of your window does not mean that nothing is happening. Bricks, mortar, rocks, trees, and other observable items in the material world do not normally react spontaneously to change under any circumstances. They will be amongst the last things to demonstrate the effects of a transformational impulse.

These forces work from within, on our higher spiritual dimensions. The first things to respond to their impulse will be us humans.

The initial changes will be felt within us. Within our souls. Within our hearts. Within our minds. The world will change from the inside out, beginning with us.

First we change. Then we change the world. We have already altered it considerably since its creation and not always for the better. We are already co-creators.

The world as we know it today is the result of a joint enterprise between humanity and the universal creator. Unfortunately, mankind's contributions do not generally reflect an awareness of a partnership of any sort, least of all divine. They demonstrate a short sighted, self centred attitude that is frequently pitted directly against the natural world rather than working in harmony with it. A sense of unity with nature is conspicuously absent. The environmental imbalances that have resulted from such disharmony are now becoming all too obvious.

As custodians of this small planet we stand accused, not just of criminal negligence, but of wanton destruction. We have plundered her natural resources with no thought to the consequences. We have seriously depleted the rain forests that generate our oxygen. We have torn a gaping hole in the ozone layer with our vain aerosol sprays. We have polluted her land, her rivers, her seas and her air with all manner of human refuse from sewage and agricultural pesticides to nuclear waste. We have hunted many of her creatures to the point of extinction. Directly and indirectly, we have wiped thousands of species from the face of the Earth. As if that isn't enough, we have stockpiled sufficient weapons to instantaneously convert the entire planet into another asteroid belt.

The powers that be obviously have their priorities right in selecting the human race to be the first to benefit from the coming transformation. If anything here on Earth needs changing, it is us. We are the only bit that does not work in total harmony with the whole.

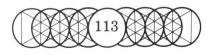

We are out of tune, not only with the Earth and the universe, but with our own inner essence, our true nature. We have yet to discover who we are and what we are doing here.

On the strength of what we've been doing so far, an apocalypse may indeed seem to be imminent. Don't delude yourself that it will be an act of God. It is far more likely to be of our own making.

As a race, we have yet to learn what the Chinese dragon men knew three thousand years ago: whatever damage we inflict upon our environment, we ultimately inflict upon ourselves. As a direct result, we are currently reaping the bitter harvest of our own thoughtless actions. Understandably, the prophets of doom have been having a field day. You will be glad to hear that I am not one of them. In fact, although the outlook may seem decidedly grim to us mere mortals, from the cosmic standpoint, everything may actually be going according to plan.

The myriad problems currently besetting humanity may well be a necessary stage in our development, part of our education, teaching us the hard way, by personal experience.

They result directly from fundamental errors in our understanding that cannot go uncorrected if we are to progress to the next evolutionary level. If they are being dramatically brought to our attention at this time, it is as a lesson to us all.

When fate decides to whack you in the face with a metaphorical custard pie, or even a bag of manure, it is not doing you a dis-service. It is presenting you with a unique opportunity to examine the situation and events leading up to it with a view to developing new insights and abilities hitherto unsuspected in your make-up.

If you react to the challenge correctly, you will not only find the solution to your problems, you will emerge from the experience a wiser, stronger, more evolved person. If not, fate will select another bag of manure and lie in wait ready to repeat the exercise as often as necessary for the lesson to sink in.

The very same processes work on a planetary scale. The Earth and its occupants are currently undergoing one such negative learning experience, a true dark age from which, hopefully, we will emerge into the light of a new era. If we have reached crisis point in an unprecedented number of areas, it is because we are being urged to recognise the error of our ways and make amends in order to continue along our correct evolutionary path.

Like errant children, we are being asked to clean up the mess in our room and to modify our behaviour before being allowed into the rest of the house. If we do not voluntarily change our ways, fate has a great many bags of manure lined up for us. The most obvious are labelled pollution, global warming, nuclear energy and war. All of these items can come in large, apocalypse-sized bags. Although the human motives behind them, lust for power, greed, hatred, envy, mistrust, fear and myopic self-interest are all just as dangerous.

Fortunately, there are forces at work in the world other than man's own destructive tendencies. They are already active within the land and

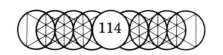

within the souls, hearts and minds of its people, urging those who are sensitive to their influence to first turn away from the brink of global catastrophe, then to re-attune ourselves, our planet and our way of life to the harmony of the universal order.

Thousands of years ago, we inhabited the spiritual dimensions of the collective unconscious as naturally as we inhabit the physical world today. We were directly attuned to our environment and the divine forces that guide us, reacting to them instinctively, just as the earth's other creatures still do. In recent millenia, our natural development has entailed a painful sense of isolation from the rest of the universe. Our collective identities, our divine origins, our sense of unity with the Earth, with the cosmos and with God have all taken a back seat while we have been engaged in the process of developing individual consciousness and self-awareness.

We have improved our intellectual capabilities at the expense of our intuition. Inner vision and imagination have taken second place to external invention. Mysticism, magic and other spiritual sciences have given way to the science and technology of the material world. In the psycho-spiritual realms to which we only have access through the inner workings of our minds, we have become like strangers, the result of a lengthy period of familiarisation with the physical world around us.

Do not misunderstand me. So far, none of this has done us any real harm. It has all been a necessary stage in our evolution. But it has served its purpose and is now coming to a natural end. We are now beginning to re-unite these two apparently opposing aspects of our nature, to become something greater than the sum of our parts.

There is far more to us humans than a physical body and a spark of consciousness. We are multi-dimensional energy beings, with infinite potential. The time has now come for those hidden dimensions of our divine essence to begin revealing themselves to us. Like lost children, we are about to discover our true heritage and claim our rightful place in the universe. Our lengthy exile from conscious unity with the cosmic order, our fall from grace, is drawing to an end. The Earth is commencing a new phase, re-aligning itself again with the divine forces of universal creation. The ancient power centres of the planet are re-activating, re-energising, re-connecting to the cosmic mains; even the ones that have been obliterated over the centuries, or are as yet undiscovered.

Some of them are identified now by the mysterious circles of flattened crops that have begun to appear in our fields. Their patterns and proportions relate directly to the ancient wisdom of sacred geometry too. They represent a vertical component in the Earth's energy grid - a part which links the energies of the Earth to the those of the universe at large. The energy spirals that form them are a direct manifestation of divine power becoming more noticeably active "On Earth as it is in heaven."

On all our subconscious levels, our planet and ourselves are gradually re-attuning to the universal harmony and the divine will. The seeds of transformation have been planted within each one of us, waiting to germinate in the light of our inner consciousness.

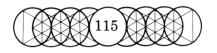

There are no exceptions to this rule. No special arrangements for Jehovah's Witnesses, Jews, Christians, Catholics, pagans, Muslims, Hindus, agnostics or anyone else. If you are a human being of any description, incarnate on the Earth now, change is inevitable. Ultimately, it involves a dramatic augmentation of human perception. To quote Gareth Knight, it entails:

" The evolution of consciousness from animal man to angelic man, from instinctual behaviour patterns to conscious intuitional modes of perception and behaviour."

Our consciousness currently functions through seven levels, the five physical senses of touch, taste, smell, sight and hearing, plus our emotions and thoughts. To simplify things a little, that reflects a three dimensional consciousness of physical, emotional and mental awareness. Gradually, this will develop into a further, fourth level of consciousness, what some of us presently call spiritual awareness, but which is actually a perception of fourth dimensional reality.

The picture you see on a television screen is not the sum total of all the programmes and channels available to you. It is just the one you're tuned to for that moment. In the same way, the world you see around you is only one of the realities open to your perception. It is all a question of attunement. Over the next couple of decades, we will all be re-tuned subconsciously to a different channel on a higher frequency.

There is a new power in the land. It flows from the very source of all life, permeating all things with a web of divine energy, consciousness and purpose. Through the star-fields of the collective mind it will implant a new vision for the future of humanity in the individual minds of those who are destined to have a powerful influence on our progress in years to come. Through the star-fields of the collective soul, it will touch the hearts of all, opening them to new levels of understanding, compassion and love.

Fear, anxiety, aggression, mistrust, hatred, despair, anger and greed will begin to be things of the past for those attuned to the higher frequencies of the divine life-force. Eventually, they will cease to exist altogether as human characteristics. They are a part of the first heaven and Earth that will pass away and be no more.

This is not a reference to the total destruction of the physical world, as the doom-mongers would have us believe, but the lowest frequencies of the planet's energy spectrum (hence " heaven and Earth," not just Earth). In particular, it is those frequencies that carry the lowest energies of the human collective unconscious. They are the planetary energy fields which have been polluted by the darkest contents of every human mind. They are an aspect of the feminine Earth Spirit, the collective soul of the planet, which has been despoiled by humanity to become the woman referred to in Revelation I7, verse 5:

" Mystery, Babylon the great,
the mother of harlots and abominations of the Earth. "

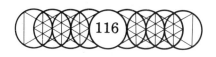

All the evil perpetrated by man upon his fellow man and upon the Earth is recorded and preserved in the inner energies of the planet's collective biosphere. It is present in the human energy spectrum and permeates the lower frequencies of the earth's pentagonal and hexagonal starfields. The symbolism of the beast of Revelation upon which Babylon sits, reinforces this notion in several ways. Its seven heads may be an indication that the beast is an aspect of man's inner energy system, with its seven chakric centres and seven levels of inner consciousness accessible through them. Its ten horns are a direct parallel with the ten points of the stellar decagram, one of the energy patterns which carry the frequencies of the human subconscious. Other references clearly support this connection between Babylon, the Beast and the human collective psyche.

" And here is the mind which has wisdom."
Revelation 17: 9.

" These (the ten horns) have one mind,
and shall give their power and strength unto the beast"
Revelation 17: 13.

"And he (the angel) said unto me, the waters that thou sawest,
where the whore sitteth, are peoples, and multitudes and nations
and tongues."
Revelation 17: 15.

Obviously, this aspect of the Earth's star-fields is not inherently evil, but as the carrier of several human subconscious frequencies, it is open to any psychic human input for good or bad, whether consciously directed into it, or spontaneously absorbed. Hence the pentagram's associations with witchcraft and, as an unbalanced, single, inverted pentagram, with the devil and satanism. Thankfully, it is now generally re-balancing to the higher universal frequencies of the Christ impulse through the ancient power centres and planetary chakras.

In these contexts, the Beast of Revelation can only be interpreted as the untamed nature of the human collective psyche. The beast that has the "number of a man" does so because it is the beast within man.

It is the unfettered remnant of the animal instinct to survive individually, whatever the cost to others. It is "the law of the jungle" ruthlessly exploited as a way of life in the soulless, concrete jungle of the modern world. It is the dark side of human nature that has turned the collective soul of the planet, the female Earth Spirit, into Babylon, the whore and;

"Habitation of devils, and hold of every foul spirit, and a cage
of every unclean and hateful bird."
Revelation 18: 2.

It seems that we have polluted our inner realms as badly as our physical world. In fact, the inner pollutants of erronous attitudes, emotions and motives is the prime causal factor behind our external problems. By and large, most of the world's worst ills are simply the physical symptoms of a sick organism with a deeply rooted, chronic affliction.

The disease, to put it bluntly, is us. Or more precisely, it is the nastiest features that afflict the human character; greed, envy, hatred, intolerance, lust for power, egoism and the shallow, short-sighted, materialistic values that deny us a spiritual reality, a sense of unity with all life and a need to care for our fellow human beings and the environment which supports us. As Martin Luther King so aptly expressed it:

"Mankind has learned to fly through the air like birds, to swim in the sea like fish. We have still to learn how to walk the Earth like brothers."

In the interests of the preservation and evolution of the species, these characteristic of human behaviour will become extinct in years to come. They are not in harmony with the incoming higher frequencies and will be increasingly difficult to sustain as time goes by.

Those unfortunate folk who currently exhibit them will have to undergo a rather dramatic personality change as they find themselves growing progressively out of tune with the spirit of the age and with their fellow human beings. From within, they will be encouraged to undergo a kind of spiritual heart transplant. The higher energies will urge them to open their hearts, at last, to some finer feelings and emotions, initiating a metaphorical change of heart on many subjects.

Those who are reluctant to abandon their anti-social ways will only be able to exhibit them in the company of people who are similarly afflicted. They will gravitate towards and gather in certain areas where the community spirit has been so badly blighted by their collective presence that it will continue to maintain them while the rest of the world's populace enjoy increasingly rewarding lifestyles. Suffering is always the price to be paid for hanging on to things that do you no good. Eventually though, these characteristics and all beings who demonstrate them will cease to exist completely. Like Homo Erectus, Neanderthal and Cro-Magnon man, they will become an extinct species.

Whether this process will occupy a sufficient length of time for these traits to die out naturally, so to speak, remains to be seen. Evolution proceeds at a relatively glacial rate compared to human activities and time scales, but, if my own experiences in recent years are anything to go by, entry into the new age of Aquarius for many people will still entail an unavoidable personal apocalypse, if not a planetary one.

The degree of trauma that your individual transformation will provoke will be in direct proportion to your reluctance to relinquish your negative characteristics. Initially, you may experience a lot of problems, emotional, psychological or physical. Don't worry. Think of it as the normal

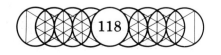

response of a faulty amplifier to an increased current. At first, you just get amplified faults. Accept it as a natural part of the healing and purification process. It is nature's way of telling you what needs to be dealt with to bring about your own re-attunement to the pulse of the universe.

The cosmic life-force is moving humanity irreversibly towards perfection. It wants you to redress your imbalances, to perfect yourself. You are part of its programme to develop the perfect human and the next major improvements to the current model are about to be implemented. With or without your conscious participation.

You cannot stand in the way of evolution. Ask any dinosaur.

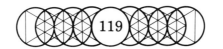

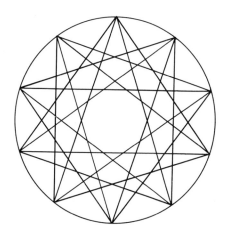

CHAPTER TEN

THE BEGINNING IS NIGH

" I, the living God, am here within you,
and within your family,
and within your neighbours,
and within your friends and enemies,
within your domestic animals
and within all the wild beasts of the Earth,
within your rivers and your seas,
within your land, your trees, your plants,
within the air that you breathe and the food that you eat.
I have always been here, but you saw me not.
Look for me and I will open your eyes to a new world.
Open your hearts to me in all you see around you
and I will open the gates of the new Jerusalem,
the gates of paradise, unto you.
You enter it not in the flesh, but in the spirit.
And the spirit you enter it in is mine;
The Holy Spirit;
The spirit of love.
Come.
Meet thy maker.
Not in death,
But in eternal life."

The new Jerusalem is a symbol of the new age. It introduces us to our spiritual dimensions, our hidden relationships to nature and the Earth, to the stones, the stars and the universe, to each other and to God. It indicates clearly that entry into the new age will not be via the blind alley of materialism or the remote control button of high technology. You enter into the spirit of it, through the portals of your individual mind and soul, into the greater awareness of their collective counterparts.

If this sounds suspiciously like some effort on your part may be required, you are not mistaken. Your personal attunement to the energies of the new age is governed by your own thoughts, actions and motivations as well as the influence of your inner spiritual energies.

Some people who are acutely aware of their spiritual existence and their relationship to the divine are already living in the new age, just as some folks insist on living in the past. It is all a matter of awareness, of where your attention is directed. For most people, the transformational forces of the new Jerusalem function only on a subconscious level, where their effects on human nature and consciousness are indirect. By developing a conscious awareness of those forces, you allow them to function at a level where their influence is far more direct and effective, not just on you, but on human nature as a whole.

The highest frequency flowing through the star-field circuits of the new Jerusalem is the power Christ drew on to work miracles, to heal the sick, make the blind see, the lame walk. Each one of us has access to that power through our spiritual energy centres, our chakras.

> *" He that believeth in me, the works that I do*
> *shall he do also; and greater works than these*
> *shall he do."*
> John 14; 12

We can allow it to heal ourselves, our fellow human beings and our blighted planet.

> *" in the midst of the street of it (the new Jerusalem),*
> *and on either side of the river, was there the tree of life,*
> *which bare twelve manner of fruits and yielded her fruit*
> *every month; and the leaves of the tree were for the healing*
> *of the nations."*
> Revelation 22; 2.

The divine life-forces supporting and sustaining all life are frequently symbolised as a "tree of life", so it is no surprise to find it used as a reference to the new Jerusalem, the most comprehensive circuit diagram of divine power ever discovered.

Anyone who feels drawn to work with these higher energies, either for their own personal attunement or for the benefit of humanity as a whole, will find the rarified spiritual atmosphere of our sacred sites the ideal place to begin. At these places, you enter an intensified spiritual energy field. Your mere presence there will allow the higher frequencies to permeate your entire being and to begin the lengthy process of harmonising your own inner energies with the divine pulse of the universe.

Find your own local power centre, whether it is your local church, a nearby hill top, a grove of trees in the local park or a listed ancient site. Then use it as a sanctuary, visiting it regularly to build up a personal relationship and resonance between yourself and its energies. Try to "tune

into" the site, sense the nature of its local guardian spirit, its connections to other sacred power centres in the vicinity, its specific function in that area and what you can do to aid that purpose. The sheer strength of the spiritual energy at some of these places greatly enhances your own ability to make a personal connection to the divine, both within yourself and in the world at large. However, there are a number of meditational techniques you can employ anywhere to enhance the contact and deepen the bonds.

Spiritual energy responds to movement, to sound and to mind, but where personal energies are concerned, most directly to breath. The latin word spiritus literally means breath of life. An empathic response between the breath that brings life-giving oxygen to our bodies and the spiritual energies that breathe life into our souls is understandable.

By the same token, the sound of the human voice, in speech, prayer, chant or song is obviously a consciously directed expression of breath and so may be used as a powerful amplifier of spiritual energy, becoming more effective as more people participate.

Your mind also has a potent link to spiritual force. The creative powers of the human mind are a reflection of the universal mind and consciousness which created it. You can think spiritual energy into existence, by liberating it onto a higher conscious level of thought and action. By using your imagination to visualise and to feel these forces entering your body through your chakras, you consciously stimulate their natural flow and enhance their effects.

When you combine this exercise with co-ordinated breathing so that you breathe the energy in, you make it doubly effective. Use both techniques regularly to open yourself to the influence of the divine forces. Literally breathe the Holy Spirit into your heart, mind and soul through your chakric centres. You can do it sitting, standing or lying down, in the privacy of your own home or in the sanctity of a holy place, as the mood takes you.

Before you begin, breathe slowly, deeply and rhythmically for several minutes to bring about a state of relaxation and to quieten the normal activity of the mind. When you feel ready, use your imagination to picture the sun that burns at the centre of the Earth, the still molten core of the planet, the source of the Earth's energy. As you slowly inhale, mentally draw this energy up through the soles of your feet into the area of your base chakra.

As you breath out, feel and visualise the energy flowing out through this chakra, opening it like a flower coming to full bloom. Repeat this as many times as you think necessary to awaken the centre to full function. Then draw the energy up to the next chakra near the navel and repeat the same process. In this way, you gradually progress to the crown chakra at the top of your head. Here you should imagine the chakra opening upwards allowing the highest energy of the divine vibration to enter your being. Feel and visualise it as an vertical column of bright light and energy shining into you, illuminating you first from above, then from within. Draw that energy down chakra by chakra, breath by breath to illuminate, cleanse, purify and heal your entire energy system. At your heart centre, realise that you have completed a great energy circuit by linking your heart to the

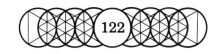

heart of the planet and the heart of the planet to the source of all life at the heart of the universe.

Mentally direct the energy and light to whichever parts of your body you feel need special attention. As you breathe it out through your chakric centres, see it re-vitalising the spiritual energy field which surrounds you until you feel like a radiant being in a globe of vibrant light and power. If you feel capable, channel that energy into the Earth through your base and through the soles of your feet, or beam it out as divine benevolence and love from your heart to the surrounding area and its inhabitants.

For some, the intensity of this light and energy imagery may be somewhat overpowering, so as an alternative, you could try to visualise and feel it as the waters of life, gently washing through your being from head to foot, cleansing your body and soul of its imperfections.

As you perform these exercises, you may feel all kinds of unusual sensations, experience flashes of insight, or even see some relevant inner imagery as the divine force touches areas of your being that require attention. Make a note of them, perhaps even keep a diary record. Over a period of time they can eventually provide a great insight into your psycho-spiritual make-up and needs.

When you are working through the solar plexus chakra, however, it is advisable to remember that it is the prime centre of subconscious psychic interaction with the human collective unconscious. Through it, you are likely to pick up intuitions, feelings and emotions from people around you, often experiencing them as vividly as if they were your own. When they are negative emotions, this can be very unpleasant, not to say disturbing. To rid yourself of them, draw them as energy up to your heart chakra to purify them with its love before expelling them through it back into the world at large. A lot of tummy troubles in psychically sensitive folk, particularly those who do not know or accept that they are psychic, is due to this centre being over-receptive. It can be helped by consciously visualising a shield, window, filter or some other barrier over the chakra to block out the lower negative influences whilst still allowing the higher spectrum of force through.

Moving up to the heart chakra for a moment, it's only fair to point out that this is another centre prone to extreme reactions. When the divine power touches your inner heart, it may unleash a flood of emotion that has been pent-up for years. If you burst into tears uncontrollably, don't worry. It's a common reaction. On the other hand, you may actually experience the force as the power of divine love emanating from the heart and source of all creation, provoking a personal feeling of intense unconditional love and well-being. Don't keep it to yourself. Radiate it from your own heart to the surrounding area and to anyone in need of its benevolent influence.

Allow the energy and its associated sensations and insights to flow and circulate through your inner being naturally by remaining calm and relaxed, breathing slowly deeply and gently until you feel that the experience is drawing to an end. Afterwards, you will need to reverse the initial technique to aid your return to a normal state of consciousness and the everyday world. Beginning at the crown chakra, breathe your own

spiritual energies which have been extended beyond their normal limits back into your physical body and contain them by visualising each chakra closing up and returning from a state of extra-sensory function to normal autonomous control. Earth yourself by feeling your feet firmly rooted to the ground. Stamp them to reinforce the idea if you feel it helps.

Once you begin to appreciate meditation as a spiritual routine, you'll discover all kinds of techniques which can be adopted or developed to suit your own personal needs. However, on a more cautionary note, as a general rule, westerners should not dabble in eastern meditational techniques which have a strong ethnic element to them unless you have a personal affinity with their origins. They are designed to facilitate contact with archetypes, energies and divinites of the eastern collective unconscious rather than their western counterparts.

Similarly, some of the more remote or ancient sacred sites may link strongly to pagan figures and deities, innerworld site guardians and other unusual psychic manifestations as a result of their previous ritual use or in some cases more recent misuse of the lower frequencies. If you can cope with such encounters, fine. If not, or if the atmosphere strikes you as being in any way odd (it may be part of the site's natural cycle), take heed and steer clear of them until you are more experienced.

Alternatively, you can learn to by-pass these images from a site's lower psychic levels and past earthly associations by simply focusing your attention on an image which has strong associations with the levels you do wish to attune to. Try a white dove of peace, the image of an angel, the Virgin Mary, or the risen Christ.

If, on the other hand, you feel inclined towards more adventurous and mystical experimentation, try meditating on the geometric patterns of the new Jerusalem. By using them as mandalas, you allow the energies to influence you directly. As you stare at them you will notice the designs constantly changing before your eyes, emphasising different energy patterns and connections. Each change corresponds to a shift in your own perception and inner energies so take it nice and easy. You don't want to blow a fuse. To attune to the Earth Goddess or any of her associated archetypes, work with the 20 pointed stellagram. The Virgin Mary seems to have some association of her own with the eight-pointed star, aligned so that two points face each point of the compass. For the inspiration of the moon goddess, the eighteen-pointed stellagram is recommended.

If you have any difficulty mastering these techniques or if meditation of any sort is all terra incognita to you, stick to basic meditational methods which concentrate on simply relaxing your physical body and focusing your attention on breathing slowly, deeply and rhythmically. By stilling the conscious mind you find peace within, re-awakening your awareness of the divine presence within yourself and eventually in everyone and everything around you. When practised regularly, that alone will be sufficient to initiate the process of personal enlightenment and transformation on an inner level for most people. From then on, it's up to you. It's not exactly a rapid process. It can take years, or even a lifetime. But once you allow the guiding forces of the universe to influence your life, you will find that your

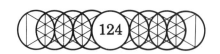

personal path of liberation gradually unfolds before you, with new revelations, insights, knowledge and experiences often turning up out of the blue.

Just like any pilgrim's progress, some stages of the journey are exceptionally demanding, while others can bring great fun or simply blinding flashes of inspiration. Ultimately, everyone's path leads back to their individual relationship with a common, universal source of being.

" The oldest wisdom in the world tells us
that we can consciously unite with the divine
whilst in the body, for this man is really born."
Rhadakrishnan.

Like the gnostics of old, you may eventually establish a personal rapport with the unity of spirit at the root of all religious experience rather than the divisive dogma of its different Earthly interpretations. " Be still and know that I am God" is no idle phrase, but a reality you can experience personally, then practice until you are perfect.

" God became man so that man can become God."
St. Athanasius.

Many people who have never discovered the art of meditation are reluctant to believe that sitting perfectly still and ostensibly doing nothing for fifteen or twenty minutes a day can achieve anything at all. In fact, impressive testimonies of its benefits for the individual can be found in almost every book on the subject.

Less well-known, even amongst experienced meditators, are its effects on the collective psyche. Everything that happens in your mind simultaneously happens in the collective mind of which yours is an intrinsic part. Every single person who consciously re-attunes to the divine presence within themselves not only begins to re-charge, re-balance and replenish their own spiritual energies, but also those of the Earth and every person upon it. In short, meditation's capacity to plug you into the collective consciousness makes it a potent tool for planetary transformation as well as personal enlightenment.

" Work on yourself and serve the world" was the motto of the grail knights. As it turns out, the two tasks are inseparable. When you do one, you automatically do both. As you change yourself, so you change those around you. As you change yourself, so you change the world.

Until I stumbled upon this realisation, I'd often wondered how the meek were going to inherit the Earth. Now, we've been given a clue. Maybe they will just quietly meditate, joining forces with the incoming energies of the new age as it increasingly takes effect on those around them, slowly making the world a more peaceful place.

Meditation applied specifically for these ends does for peace what sneezing does for the common cold virus. It makes it highly contagious, affecting everyone and everything in our immediate vicinity, through our

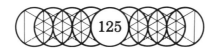

constant interaction with the energy star-fields of the earth and humanity which envelop us.

Once you understand these natural interactions with your psycho-spiritual dimensions and their collective counterparts, you can start to become an active agent of transformation, automatically aligning yourself with the forces of creation and allowing them to work through you for the benefit of mankind. In this new capacity, you can then begin to apply yourself to the task of consciously re-activating and amplifying the esoteric functions of our sacred sites as centres of divine power.

Initially, this entails nothing more than your conscious acknowledgement that there is more to them than meets the eye. Think beyond their physical facade as churches, abbeys, cathedrals, temples, synagogues, prehistoric stones, ancient monuments, sacred wells, holy hills or whatever. What they look like is unimportant. They are all spiritual power stations, even the ones that are no more than a pile of long-neglected, old ruins. The life-support system of the universe flows through them all, energising and animating the Earth and everything upon it, maintaining and regulating every life-cycle under its autonomous control, radiating the ultimate in benificent influences to the surrounding area. It can be seen, heard, sensed and dowsed by many people who have developed a personal affinity to it.

Even if you have no personal sensitivity for these matters at all, try to be aware that divine energies do emanate invisibly from these places, their currents ebbing and flowing in harmony with the seasonal cycles of the Earth which in turn are a reflection of celestial rhythms. Your conscious acknowledgement of those forces releases them into the collective energy fields of the race and of the planet at a far more effective level of action.

Every single person who realises that their parish church or some other local site is a centre of spiritual power, stimulates and amplifies that power by raising it from the realms of indirect subconscious influence to a more direct level of effect with the energy fields of the Earth and human consciousness.

If your intentions are pure, a variety of visualisation techniques can be employed to activate, amplify and direct these spiritual forces with enormous impact on the energies inherent in the surrounding area and its communities. Bless the site verbally with any words you feel appropriate, or use this simple prayer;

Bless this centre of divine power.
May its energies be restored to their full power and glory,
balanced in perfect harmony with the divine will.
May they flow forth from here
carrying the power of light, life, peace, love and joy
into the hearts, minds and souls of all mankind.
May they heal humanity.
May they heal the Earth .
May the divisions between the worlds of man,
nature and divinity, be healed.

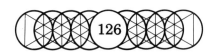

Visualisation is vital to reinforce your intent and to empower it on the inner planes. Imagine the sites being energised by a vertical column of divine power from above. See it building up so that they become ablaze with spiritual light and energy. Visualise if you can, that energy, gently radiating out to uplift the spirits of all within its sphere of influence, literally doing a power of good. Imagine it opening their hearts, souls and minds to the light and love of their creator, awakening them to the presence of the divine within themselves and within the world around them. Reinforce and amplify its effects by visualising those, too. Think of it as the power and spirit of Christ, doing what Christ would do himself, healing the sick in mind, body and spirit, supporting, strengthening and protecting the weak, provoking a change of heart and mind in the misguided, righting wrongs and upholding justice.

Those who have felt this power personally actually experience it as a sensation of intense unconditional love, the love of the universal being for all its creations and children, no matter how wayward. To maximise its impact, project it in the same form, as intense unconditional love. Imagine how the sun might feel, sitting at the centre of the solar system, selflessly beaming its light, love and energy to its offspring the planets. That's the kind of feeling you have to try to generate.

A prolonged and repeated input of supercharged spiritual love and energy into an area can work miracles. You can change the emotional climate. Where fear, anxiety, violence and oppression prevail, you can begin to create an atmosphere of peace and trust. In areas ravaged by thoughtless planning, years of neglect, or rampant anti-social elements, you can literally rebuild and restore the community spirit. In places plagued by crime and violence, you can defuse the criminal mentality by generating an atmosphere that is less conducive to the activities of thieves, muggers and vandals.

Of course, there is also an enormous amount of more practical work to be done in all these areas of endeavor, but as you well know, in the right atmosphere, everyone is motivated to work better, think more positively and to co-operate more effectively.

That vital ingredient is now available on a global scale to spur on all those who are working in the spirit of the new age, to repair the damage mankind has inflicted upon the world and to build it anew.

" the leaves of the tree are for the healing of the nations."
Revelation 22: 2.

Try to incorporate these exercises in community and planetary healing into your prayers, your religious services, your meditations and other spiritual practices. If you can, form a group that meets regularly to heal, harmonise and spiritually awaken your local community. The addresses of a few organisations, like Fountain International, who are already involved in this kind of activity and can offer some further help and advice, are given at the end of the book.

What you visualise in your meditations will one day become reality. All you create in your individual mind, you allow the the universal life-force to create in the collective mind and in the world around you, first on the inner realms, but ultimately at a level that will be perceived by every man, woman and child on the planet. In this way, you can transmute the human collective unconscious and raise its main operational level from the solar plexus to the heart chakra, replacing our self-centred society with a more caring, heart-centred society.

As I said, you can work miracles. You can change the world. Yes. You. Not too much to ask, is it ?

Already, thousands of souls are awakening to the realisation that "the redemption of the fallen planet", as Sir George Trevelyan calls it, is underway. In the Hopi Indian prophecies, these enlightened folk are referred to as the Warriors of the Rainbow, people of all races, colours and creeds who will come together when the earth is dying, to heal it and restore it, not only to its former glory, but to its rightful place in the universal order. They have elected to be born on the Earth at this time, not just to be present at the birth of a new age, but to actively assist with that birth. Many of them are already aware of their spiritual path, the demands that this age places upon them and of the individual tasks that lie before them. Many more will have been gently alerted to their true nature by the catalyst of this book. To them, its contents will not have come as a revelation. Instead it will have all seemed reassuringly familiar, like something they already knew deep inside, but had long forgotten. Read and remember.

Regardless of the Rainbow Warriors' impressive purpose here on Earth, it would be wholly inaccurate to portray them as some kind of spiritual fifth cavalry who will save us from our own folly by riding to the rescue at the last minute. The majority are ordinary people with ordinary lives. They just happen to be aware of their spiritual identity and potential, as well as the fact that we must all, as individuals, shoulder the burden of responsibility for the current state of the planet, doing all we can personally to reverse the damage.

In the cosmic scheme of things, ordinary people will be able to change the world far more dramatically than its "important" leaders. The spirit of the age influences the populace at large far easier than it can affect the near inflexible doctrines of party politics.

The greatest transformation the world has known will be accomplished not by its presidents, prime ministers and politicians, but by ordinary people lending the weight of their incarnate spiritual presence to sway the collective psyche of the planet to the divine will of our disincarnate creator.

As each additional human being re-attunes, it will become progressively easier for others to resonate harmoniously with them, thanks to the phenomenon of rhythmic entrainment, the tendency of all identical things in motion to eventually harmonise their actions. Actually, rhythmic entrainment on a grand scale is an appropriate, if somewhat oversimplified, explanation of what is now happening in the relationship

between the universe, the Earth and its inhabitants. We are all beginning to move together, as one. As more and more people in the community become spiritually aware and as that awareness increases, they will precipitate a chain reaction that uplifts the collective consciousness of the entire planet to the same heightened levels of perception. A point of critical mass will eventually be reached, triggering a massive shift in global consciousness as the human element of the Earth's energies shift the entire planet to a higher band of frequencies. Despite the fact that this will undoubtably affect every living soul on the entire planet, the vast majority of people do not necessarily need to have the vaguest inkling of its possible occurance.

This monumental accomplishment can be engineered by a relatively small percentage of the planetary populace, a resonant minority, which in layman's terms, is a number of people who are already attuned to the higher frequncies of the new age and functioning in harmony with them. Rhythmic entrainment itself does the rest, rapidly gaining pace as its momentum builds.

Exactly how many souls constitute a resonant minority in the Earth's collective psyche, or indeed how long in might be before the meek gain their minority influence on planetary progress, are at the moment inestimable and not something I would care to guess at. But once word gets around, I have a feeling we won't have too long to wait. We live in an age of mass media and global communication that would have been unimaginable in Christ's era. At no other time in history has there been the potential to make knowledge available to the world's population on the scale we can today. In my opinion, anyone alive and in reasonable health now will live to see an astonishing escalation of change in the world, marked by a dramatic transformation of human perception, thought and accomplishment over the next couple of decades and leading to a much fuller understanding of our psycho-spiritual dimensions, their potential, the forces and beings who inhabit them.

There are thousands of spiritually attuned souls upon the Earth already. You may be the one additional person needed to tip the balance in the collective consciousness of humanity, by opening your inner perception to the reality of the spiritual realms, allowing the divine powers and hierarchies within them conscious expression in the experiential world.

The beginning is nigh. Global transformation and the spiritualisation of matter is an imminent possibility. The floodgates of divine force are waiting to be fully opened to allow the waters of life to complete the cleansing and purification of this planet and its populace which they have already begun.

Mother Earth, through her sacred sites, is busy re-establishing contact with her children, to alert them to her predicament, to enlist their aid in her healing and purification so that the collective soul of the Earth, the Earth Spirit, may become the bride of Christ. When that happens, her impure aspect, Babylon the whore, the personification of corrupt human

energy fields, will pass below our levels of awareness to be replaced at the top end of the scale by a higher frequency band and a whole new area of perception.

The human race may at last make the quantum leap to sixth and seventh senses, to fourth dimensional reality, in full consciousness. Technology may go psi-tronic. Telepathy, clairvoyance and other psychic faculties now dormant or underdeveloped may become commonplace, enabling the new Jerusalem, the Kingdom of God, to be founded upon the Earth in a form accessible to all enlightened beings.

The second coming of Christ may then actually come as a conscious manifestation of the world soul fully able to interact directly with human consciousness. It would bring with it full awareness of the divine hierarchies of nature and the higher realms. Who knows, maybe man will once again walk the Earth in the company of angels? When depends largely on us, but the process has already commenced. The divine plan is underway.

London and Great Britain as a whole are clearly destined to play an important role in that plan. In the past, of course, Britain has already given birth to the new worlds of North America, Australasia and the now fragmented British Commonwealth. Although all of her former colonies are now self-governing, there still exists, on the non-physical realms, strong bonds between them.

There are qualities peculiar to the British national spirit, principally, a unique sense of justice, tolerance and fair-play, which have gone forth into the rest of the world and been sown as seeds in the spirit of many other nations. They have already brought far-reaching changes to the world. Now they will evolve to carry the finer qualities of the spirit of Christ and the new age, to bring change on a much wider scale.

The new age is not for London, Great Britain or the English-speaking world alone. It is for the entire world. London is simply one of several planetary power centres awakening to conscious activity. Like the new Jerusalem, it is very definitely a model of life on a global scale. It is a cosmopolitan city, inhabited by all races, colours and creeds, with residents and visitors from every possible country. It is a focal point of global consciousness, even before you consider its possible connections to a planetary grid of star, soul and mind fields.

Its role as a centre of world power and influence is assured, although not in the same way as it has been at certain moments in its history, through economic or political power, subjugation and force of arms. In spiritual matters, one must lead as Christ did, by example and by openly providing support, encouragement, guidance and knowledge for the benefit of others.

The spirit of the new age is, above all else, one of peaceful co-operation and mutual understanding. It offers humanity the opportunity to begin, once again, working in harmony with the forces of creation. It asks each one of us to grasp that opportunity personally; to consciously re-establish the links to our divine origins and in doing so, activate a power that can transform both ourselves and our small planet. It asks world

governments to attune to and be guided by their national spirit, the spirit of their land and people, to work in harmony with the planetary soul and the divine universal order, " for the healing of the nations."

Remember that the world's greatest leaders have always themselves been led by a vision. Allow your imagination to be fired with a vision of the utopia humanity could build working in co-operation with the forces of creation. Let that vision be born in your mind; a dream of a what the future might hold for the human race when we begin to exploit our divine potential.

Then, live the dream.

And did those feet in ancient time
walk upon England's mountain's green ?
And was the holy Lamb of God
on England's pleasant pastures seen ?

And did the countenance divine
shine forth upon our clouded hills ?
and was Jerusalem builded here
among these dark satanic mills ?

Bring me my bow of burning gold,
Bring me my arrows of desire,
Bring me my spear, O, clouds unfold,
Bring me my chariot of fire.

I will not cease from mental fight,
Nor shall my sword sleep in my hand,
Till we have built Jerusalem,
in England's green and pleasant land.

William Blake.

IN EVERY END THERE IS A NEW BEGINNING.

Further copies of this book are available direct from Hermitage Publishing, P.O. Box 1383, London N14 6LF. Please send SAE for order form.

BIBLIOGRAPHY

On subjects where I have only been able to write a single chapter, others have written an entire book. Here are some of them;

THE GEOMETRY OF ART AND LIFE by MATILA GHYKA. Dover Books.

SACRED GEOMETRY by NIGEL PENNICK. Turnstone Press.

THE DIVINE PROPORTION by H.E. HUNTLEY. Dover Books.

THE MYSTERIES OF KING'S COLLEGE CHAPEL by NIGEL PENNICK. Aquarian Press Ltd.

TIME STANDS STILL by KEITH CRITCHLOW. Gordon Fraser.

SACRED GEOMETRY, PHILOSOPHY AND PRACTICE by ROBERT LAWLOR. Thames and Hudson.

ORDER IN SPACE by KEITH CRITCHLOW. Thames and Hudson.

THE POWER OF LIMITS (Proportional harmonies in nature, art and architecture) by GYOGY DOCZI. Shambhala Publications, Boston, USA.

THE EARTH SPIRIT, ITS WAYS, ITS SHRINES, ITS MYSTERIES by JOHN MICHELL. Thames and Hudson.

THE LIVING EARTH MANUAL OF FENG SHUI by STEPHEN SKINNER. Routledge and Kegan Paul.

THE ANCIENT SCIENCE OF GEOMANCY by NIGEL PENNICK. Thames and Hudson.

NEEDLES OF STONE by TOM GRAVES. Turnstone Press.

GAIA by J.E. LOVELOCK. Oxford University Press.

CITY OF REVELATION by JOHN MICHELL. Thames and Hudson.

THE DIMENSIONS OF PARADISE by JOHN MICHELL. Thames and Hudson.

A VISION OF THE AQUARIAN AGE by SIR GEORGE TREVELYAN. Coventure Ltd, London.

OPERATION REDEMPTION by SIR GEORGE TREVELYAN. Turnstone Press.

VISION, THE STARSEED TRANSMISSIONS AND TERRA CHRISTA; three books by KEN CAREY, all published by Starseed publishing Ltd.

SOME USEFUL ORGANISATIONS:

FOUNTAIN INTERNATIONAL: A charity concerned with planetary and community healing applied directly through the Earth's energy fields, its focal centres and connecting alignments; P.O. BOX 915, SEAFORD, EAST SUSSEX, BN25 ITW.

FOUNTAIN LONDON, The London group of Fountain International, PO Box 1383, London N14 6LF.

THE LUCIS TRUST, Two of its activities- WORLD GOODWILL and THE TRIANGLES NETWORK - are both directly concerned with planetary transformation: SUITE 54, 3 WHITEHALL COURT, LONDON SWIA 2EF.

THE ORDER OF BARDS, OVATES AND DRUIDS, 260 KEW ROAD, RICHMOND, SURREY, TW9 3EG. The traditional ancient wisdom of the British Isles.

THE WREKIN TRUST. RUNNINGS PARK. CROFT BANK, WEST MALVERN, WORCS. WR 14 4BP.

Please enclose an S.A.E if requesting information from any of the above sources.